*Reinventing
Womanhood*

Reinventing
Womanhood

Carolyn G. Heilbrun

 W · W · NORTON & COMPANY   NEW YORK

Part of Chapter 3 appeared, in a somewhat different
form, in *From Parnassus: Essays in Honor of
Jacques Barzun*, edited by Dora B. Weiner and William
R. Keylor (New York: Harper & Row, 1976).
Part of Chapter 6 appeared, in a somewhat different
form, in *Critical Inquiry,* Winter 1978.

"Relearning the Alphabet P,Q" by Denise Levertov,
Relearning the Alphabet. Copyright © 1970 by Denise
Levertov Goodman. Reprinted by permission of New Directions.

"Housewife" from *All My Pretty Ones* by Anne Sexton
Copyright © 1961, 1962 by Anne Sexton
Reprinted by permission of Houghton Mifflin Company

Excerpts from "Cinderella" from *Transformations* by Anne Sexton
Copyright © 1971 by Anne Sexton
Reprinted by permission of Houghton Mifflin Company

Library of Congress Cataloging in Publication Data
Heilbrun, Carolyn G
  Reinventing womanhood.
  Includes bibliographical references and index.
  1. Women—Psychology. 2. Sex role. 3. Women in
literature. 4. Fiction—Women authors—History and
criticism. I. Title.
HQ1206.H43   1979   301.41 ' 2   78-25607
ISBN 0-393-01210-7
  2 3 4 5 6 7 8 9 0

To
Emily, Margaret, and Robert
with love and admiration

Contents

Acknowledgments   9
1 Personal and Prefatory   15
2 Woman as Outsider   37
3 Women Writers and Female Characters: The
  Failure of Imagination   71
4 Search for a Model: Female Childhood   93
5 Search for a Model: History and Literature   125
6 Marriage and Family   171
7 The Claims of Woman   199
  Notes   213
  Selective Bibliography   229
  Index   237

Acknowledgments

The essay that follows will, I hope, make clear how great is my reliance on the work and courage of those who have preceded me. Although I have tried to mention my intellectual debts, where I was aware of them, I fear that some have, nonetheless, been neglected. I hope that anyone whose work I have used but failed to mention here will recognize and accept my gratitude.

I have received much support and encouragement in the writing of this book. A Rockefeller Foundation Humanities Fellowship enabled me to take a year's leave from teaching; my Fellowship at the Radcliffe Institute for Independent Study offered me the ideal ambience in which to work. I am particularly grateful to those who directed the Institute in my year there, and to those, mentioned and unmentioned, who offered me conversation and encouragement. I am grateful, too, for new friends from that time: Grace Mojtabai, novelist; Felicia Bonaparte, professor and literary critic; Grace Baruch and Rosalind Barnett, psychologists.

While in Cambridge, I benefited immeasurably from membership in two seminars: the Workshop on Female Psychology at the Boston Psychoanalytic Institute, where Dr. Malkah Notman and others offered me a rare opportunity to study women and psychoanalysis; and the Brandeis Seminar, Women: Work and Personality in the Middle Years, where I learned from outstanding scholars in several disciplines.

My debt to those who read and advised on earlier drafts of this book is enormous. None of them, of course, is necessarily in agreement with what remains. Tom Driver, my oldest and most constant friend, remained constant in the face of many drafts and permutations. Helene Moglen offered support and criticism of an especially vital and necessary kind. Thomas Sternau, once a week, on bicycles and off, encouraged the author and offered her numerous kindnesses, great and small, in connection with this book. Anne Barstow and Judith Jordan read the manuscript and instructed and emboldened its author. Joan Ferrante's intelligent reading of this work was of great value; here, as elsewhere, her courage encouraged me. My father, supportive as always, read what I had written and, because of the exigencies of our various vacations, met me in Plymouth, New Hampshire (where neither of us had ever been), to offer me, as he so often has before, his generous confidence, his wisdom, his knowledge, and lunch.

My research assistants in 1977–78, Alice Beebe and Nancy McCarthy, undertook bewildering tasks with intelligence and expediency.

My husband, Jim, has encouraged my work and edited it since long before our children were born. His labors on this book have been greater than ever. We have been equal partners in marriage, in support for the work each has undertaken, and in the upbringing of our children, now grown, to whom this book is lovingly offered.

Reinventing
Womanhood

1

Personal and Prefatory

I was in my fiftieth year when I began this book: for me
a time of flowering. A friend wrote to me at Cambridge,
after we had dined in New York: "You are in your
prime." Women seldom think of themselves as in their
prime at fifty, but I think it is often so. (Charlotte Perkins
Gilman wrote: "One day the girls were discussing what
age they would rather be, for life. Most of them agreed
on eighteen, which many of them were at that time.
When they asked me I said fifty. They didn't believe it.
'Why?' they demanded. 'Because,' I explained, 'when I'm

fifty, people will respect my opinions if they are ever going to, and I shall not be too old to work.' " She remembered this when starting the *Forerunner* at fifty.)[1]

I was devoting myself to a task for which my life had prepared me, (but this is no doubt always true of welcome tasks). I wished to name, if I could, those strictures not wholly societal or cultural that inhibit women from the full formation of a self. Obviously, there were many ways in which I was not professionally qualified for this task, but I had come to recognize a unique qualification: I felt that, unlike so many of the women I had read of and known personally, I had been born a feminist and never wavered from that position. I do not mean, of course, that I expressed feminist views in the dreary masculinist years after World War II. But I never denied the pain to myself, nor lied about my anger. The formation of this kind of feminist has perhaps received too little attention, particularly since psychologists and psychoanalysts have long been accustomed to dismiss the condition—perhaps because of its rarity—with a dirty name.

We are, for example, only now beginning to understand that the sanctification of motherhood, which prevented mothers from ever admitting to feelings of ambivalence toward their children, is not necessarily good for the child but may induce profound anxiety. Thus I can only now recognize how clear had been my mother's message about the importance of autonomy for women, clear and free of the ambiguity of most such messages from mothers to daughters. She seems to me, in retrospect, almost unique in her honesty, her ability to describe her pain, her subtle refusal to induce me to share it. She spoke to me of what she knew, of what, through great suffering, she had concluded. But she was never free to act on her own knowledge. I believe that had there been a woman's movement during her lifetime, some form of group support from women, she might have found the impulse to action. None such existed. In the thirties came the depression, in the forties war, and after the war, the return to the feminine mystique. Her childhood, poor but with that "upward" aspiration to a "higher" class, is almost a model of how convention imprisons women. She achieved the status she sought, but never denied the burden of futility she carried with her until her death. Her lasting gift to me was a message remarkably clear, uncontradictory: be independent, make your own way, do not pay with your selfhood for male admiration and approval: the price is too high. Most mothers give a double message: succeed, but not at the price of imperiling your "feminine allure." Mine did not.

I was, moreover, now, at fifty, provided with the ideal conditions for the work I had undertaken. Our children were in college; I had in some measure resigned responsibility for their destinies, not, of course, as far as money or affection or readiness for consultation was concerned, but my husband and I had quite consciously, when the youngest reached college age, abdicated any further day-to-day responsibility for them. My marriage, probably the single most fortunate factor in my life, allowed itself to develop into new forms and patterns, both of us discovering new individuality and intimacy. In having been made a Fellow of the Radcliffe Institute for Independent Study in 1976–77, I found myself simultaneously endowed with three rare blessings: I was placed in ideal working conditions; I was, for the first time in my life, part of a community of professional women; and I had the opportunity to learn from highly competent and informed people in all disciplines the fruits of their studies of women.

At that particular moment in my life, the fact that I was Jewish seemed to have less than nothing to do with the work I had undertaken. Of course, a significant proportion of the Fellows at the Radcliffe Institute were Jews, a fact I noticed without asking why I did so. An observation, I would have said, made without an effort at perception. But as I recalled memories of my years at Wellesley, my Jewishness came to consciousness.

Because my thirtieth class reunion was looming, I was invited to several meetings of my nearby Wellesley classmates who had heard I was at Radcliffe. It became clear that Wellesley had always been, in the nicest way, anti-Semitic. I was told, truthfully or not, that some of its former administrators had been notorious for this attitude. Wellesley had largely ignored me since my graduation, giving its attention, or so it seemed to me, to those of its graduates who pursued domestic and volunteer careers with a besotted devotion to ladylike attitudes and the mindless cheer of the lower half of a two-person career—for example, "We have just moved with our seven children, two dogs, guinea pigs, and the new addition to our family, a large turtle, to an igloo on an ice flow where Dick hopes to study frozen minnows." Its faculty, some of whom I had recently met, seemed to me chiefly to regret that they were not in an institution that taught males. Certainly, for a women's college, Wellesley was marvelously uncommitted to the problems of women in our time, at least as I conceived of them.[2]

One day, returning from a Wellesley encounter, I jokingly remarked to the Dean of the Radcliffe Institute that I had always assumed that Wellesley ignored me because I was a feminist. Now, I had discovered, Wellesley had ignored me because I was a Jew. This was a joke and she, a WASP, found it witty. The significance for me of that moment, only later recognized, was that for the first time the two terms had come together: feminist and Jew.

In that same year two widely publicized events occurred, both literary, both significant for me. The first was *Roots,* a book by an American Black who had set out to discover his roots in Africa. The second was *World of Our Fathers* (the title was much commented upon at the Radcliffe Institute), which I decided to read for reasons that now seem to me odd, to say the least. I did not read *Roots,* nor did I see the television program made from it or hear any of the author's lectures, which were reported as remarkably effective. But the question of "roots" was catapulted into my life. It seemed to me that every young woman feminist had suddenly developed an overwhelming interest in her "roots." My lack of interest in my own roots was absolute and this was not a pretense. As far as I could see, my parents' roots consisted precisely in their severing of them. My father and mother had cut themselves off from their past. Like Gatsby, my father had been his own creation. If I had roots, they were in his childhood and early struggles, in my mother's clean separation from her family and past. Where in Europe and America any of their forebears had lived seemed to have much less to do with me than where Jane Austen had lived. Indeed the first time I had visited Bath, England, I had had the sense of coming home. My father had, in effect, said to me: "We've got nothing to look back to. It's up to us to be ancestors."[3]

I read Howe's *World of Our Fathers* because of two luncheon conversations I had during a visit to New York from Cambridge. The first, with close friends who happen not to be Jewish, evoked from one of them the statement that she did not like peasants or the lower classes generally, thought that lack of culture showed, and why should she pretend otherwise? She is in no way a snob, and it was the sort of statement friends can make to one another without fear of being misunderstood. But I realized suddenly that I did not agree with her. "I'm a peasant," I said. "I was scraped off the Lower East Side." "Nonsense," she said, but disproved not my facts, but her prejudice.

My second lunch was with my friend Tom Driver, theologian and sustainer. He and I talked, not for the first time, about the pains of contemplating the woman's movement in its current down phase. I mentioned the difficulty experienced by many committed feminists who were not lesbians, and who received support, ironically enough, chiefly from their husbands and male friends: their women friends tended to be either antistraight, or antifeminist, at least at that time. He admitted this difficulty, which he had, indeed, observed before, but mentioned that some of those women in the Church who had been the most courageous in the struggle for a female priesthood had been, in their early years, homosexual. Perhaps, he suggested, it was their experience as lesbians that gave them the courage to be feminists. To be a feminist one had to have had an experience of being an outsider more extreme than merely being a woman. Was that possible?

Had I been an outsider? Slowly, for Tom's insights are of the percolating rather than the instant variety, I began to understand that having been a Jew, however unobserved that identification was, however fiercely I had denied the adamant anti-Semitism all around me as I grew up—still, having been a Jew had made me an outsider. It had permitted me to be a feminist.

As this insight made its slow way into my consciousness, I realized why I had said, with some hyperbole, but not much, that I had been scraped off the Lower East Side. My father, since the death of my mother a few years ago, had been telling me, in his mourning, more stories of his early youth. He had never, thank God, been a reminiscer or a teller of anecdotes, both forms of counterconversation from which I violently recoil. He had been, as a boy, as poor as it is possible to be and not actually starve to death. His mother had never spoken English. His sisters had been doomed. He had been saved only by an occasional teacher, here and there, and by his own brilliance and determination. He was early disenchanted with the whole culture from which he had come, with its ignorance, its illiteracy, and what he early considered its rigid, distorted beliefs. Much that I had been told over the years but had carefully failed to remember, came back to me. My father had grown up, in fact, not on the Lower East Side of New York but in New Jersey. Apart from that, he had lived the hard early life I would discover in Howe's book.

Now, of course, I had to read Howe's book to test my response to my father's memories set forth objectively. I thought the book excellent, well-written, and prudent in its judgments. Only in its minimal consideration of women, its constant lapses into the male noun (not the universal) as expressive of Jewish experience, did its judgment fail, as indeed Jewish judgment had always failed when contemplating women. So Howe used the phrase "obscure men" for his final sentence; his title told us it was a book not about parents, but about fathers, and the ultimate praise he had for our mothers was as "sustaining women." *World of Our Fathers* helped me to understand that if Jews were outsiders, women were outsiders among Jews.

I have decided—and the decision was not an easy one —that I could not speak of the problems of women today without speaking of my own life. Through most of my career as a professor of English literature, the prevailing literary cult has dictated that the personal be subdued. I have been a most eager and persistent follower of this ideal. Professionally trained in the so-called New Criticism, that close attention to the text that denies the relevance of any factors outside it, I found that this criticism nicely reinforced my need for impersonality. New Criticism, while often exaggerated, was not, I still believe, bad training for the reading and teaching of literature. Yet I now see that its overpowering appeal for me was that it not only allowed but demanded separation between the personality and the intellect, between, in T.S. Eliot's words, the person who suffers and the artist who creates. That I managed to keep my personal and professional lives so separated permitted me to survive: as a Jew at Wellesley in the late forties, and as a woman at Columbia in the fifties and sixties. My job, as I saw it, was to struggle through to the greatest accomplishment of which I was capable, ignoring, as far as possible, both my Jewishness and my femaleness. Which is not to say that I denied either. What I denied was the power they had to limit my *self*-development, to force me humbly, rather than arrogantly, to suffer.

Being a woman and a Jew were in no way of comparable importance in my life. The first was infinitely more pervasive; not only because it was impossible to deny or change, but also because I recognized the condition of femaleness to be for me that which Yeats described as the greatest obstacle to achievement one might confront without despair. Being female was sufficiently difficult, moreover, to counterbalance the myriad blessings heaped upon me by fortune. I was endowed with opportunity and the intelligence to use it and, above all, with parents for whom I was at once the absolutely cherished and absolutely unplanned-for only child, a combination whose strength we are only now beginning to understand.

Probably because of my parents' attitude toward Jewishness, being Jewish was for me altogether unreal. I practiced what I have since learned to call denial. To do this at the time of Adolf Hitler may seem improbable at best, but for me as for many, Nazism was so unbelievable that it was many years before I could come to grips with it. The anti-Semitism I faced as a child, apart from the Irish girls on the side streets who would scream epithets at me that I thought demented, was so genteel as to be wholly lost on me. I was given, that is, the opportunity to ignore it, and so I did. That we, my parents and I, did not move wholly into the gentile world was the result of the Holocaust. For a time I believed, mysteriously, that my mother was not Jewish at all.

Contemplating this in my fiftieth year, I recognized for the first time the degree to which women have been outsiders in ways unique to them. Black women are thus peculiarly vulnerable: they are the objects both of racism and sexism. What has not perhaps been equally emphasized is the possibility that that very condition has enabled them to succeed where black men have failed. The strength of women throughout the black experience has too often been distorted in order to illuminate the perils of black manhood rather than the strengths of black womanhood. This, like so many casually accepted patriarchal judgments of our time, has been reinforced by the reluctance of many people openly to recognize the accomplishments, both familial and professional, of Black women. From an experience in no way comparable to theirs in its degree of hardship, I was able to guess at those conditions that had made their achievement possible.

It seemed to me, furthermore, essential to discover, if I could, why the woman's movement had been ready to defeat itself after each flowering with so little help from the opposition. Each cycle of progress for women seems to end after a decade or two with precious little real advance toward equality. The complacency in women that a few steps forward induces drains the movement of its energy. Progress halts, or is even reversed.

Two strategies, conscious or otherwise, play a part in halting women's advance. These are tokenism and its inevitable concomitant, the bonding of females with males. Tokenism allows males to use one woman, or a few, to protect themselves against the claims for equal representation in their ranks. Established males discover, moreover, that they can count on the token women of achievement to isolate themselves from other women, from the causes of women, and from identification with women. Co-opting radicals is, I suppose, a well-known technique for defeating them.

Let us look, for a moment, at the eleven women who, after years of fruitless struggle, found the courage to grasp their share in the priesthood of the Episcopal Church from the reluctant or recalcitrant males who had, until that time, entirely comprised it. The methods these women used—trying every possible process within the organization of the Church, realizing eventually that the patience prescribed for so many years was to lead only to more patient waiting—these methods led, finally, to the ordination of women. True, that ordination frac-

tured the Church. Any change forced upon a long-estab-
lished, self-satisfied, self-protective institution will disrupt and divide it. But, to argue from that result to the
condemnation of every fundamental change is to refute
the history of the Reformation itself. When another generation has passed, the Episcopal Church will again be
united, the ordination of women a fact, marked by an
historical occasion.

What has happened, even so far, in the Episcopal
Church? Women, their right to the priesthood won, are
now attending divinity and theological seminaries in
preparation for ordination. But they arrive counseled by
the bishops who appointed them to avoid the feminist
women among the original eleven. Clutching their "femininity" and the instructions of the male establishment,
the young women for whom the priesthood was won
deny that they are feminist, eschew activism, and wish to
disappear, unnoticed, into the male structure. They do
not follow the first women priests with pride, even denying them publicly.

Why does this inevitably happen? Why is every gain
women make followed by a fearful step backward into the
shadow of male protection? Women have conspired in
the (perhaps unconscious) policy of the male establishment to let a few women in—more, perhaps, in times of
feminist pressure—but few enough so that when the inevitable female retreat occurs, the male establishment
will be left essentially unchanged in its evident maleness.

In 1977, women working at the United Nations were
being subjected to a considerable degree of sexual
harassment, and did not know how to deal with it because of their fear of losing not only their jobs, but their
temporary residence in the United States. Shirley Haz-
zard, novelist and former member of the U.N. Secretar-

iat, suggested to them that their plan, a resolution from an ad hoc committee, would probably not get results. She proclaimed (to great applause but, one assumes, little action) that the way for women to stop sexual harassment is to support one another. "Whatever the nature of the injustice, there should be a group of women to whom one can go for support so the complainant does not feel isolated. There must be a show of solidarity."[4]

A show of solidarity. When have women shown this, outside the few intense decades of feminist activity in history and then only among less than a majority of women? Support systems, or networks of women, have, for the most part, operated in the crises of the conventional womanly life, birth, death, imposed loneliness, but they have rarely encouraged greater female autonomy. How much nearer today are we to living with the possibility of women occupying half of the world's positions because they are half the population? The very idea strikes many women as fantasy, and a threatening fantasy at that.

The failure of woman's movements, past and present, to retain the momentum of the years of highest accomplishment can be attributed to three causes: the failure of women to bond; the failure of women to imagine women as autonomous; and the failure of even achieving women to resist, sooner or later, the protection to be obtained by entering the male mainstream. Among these causes, the failure of women to find "support systems" among themselves is certainly close to the heart of the problem. How often male leaders in the academic community have remarked to me that their wives, professional or not, can't see anything in "women's lib," (beyond of course equal pay for equal work) and, anyhow, prefer the company of men. Obviously, it is difficult in a hierarchical society to bond with the powerless against those in power, particularly when the aphrodisiac of power is an added allure.

Could anyone imagine a Black organization that refused to concern itself with Black problems, a Jewish organization that refused to concern itself with Jewish problems, a Swedish organization that would have nothing in particular to do with Swedish problems? Yet such, was the attitude of the League of Women Voters, for example, which from its inception until it felt the pressures of the current movement eschewed all questions concerned exclusively with women and refused to back candidates because of their stand on women's issues. The National Council of Jewish Women (or Catholic Women) is devoted to Jewish (or Catholic) women's concerns, which may be more nurturing or directed at children and families than would the concerns of a similar men's organization, but never for one moment has it conceived of itself as concerned with women themselves, with problems, for example, of rape, unwanted pregnancy, suffrage, marital rights, or the ownership of property by women. The very idea of taking a stand on women's issues strikes the women members of such organizations as ludicrous. (The condition of women, unlike that of Blacks, has never been made a central political concern in the United States.)

While I was at the Radcliffe Institute, the *Boston Globe* ran an article bearing the headline: "Four Harvard Women Enter All-male Bastion but Not as Feminists."[5] The all-male bastion was Rhodes Scholarships, founded seventy-four years ago and admitting women for the first time that year. Asked whether, as one of the first women ever given a Rhodes Scholarship, she was a feminist, one

of the Harvard seniors replied: "I guess I don't see myself as a feminist. I've never had to come to terms as a
minority because I have not been discriminated against.
I guess there is a problem. I haven't come in contact with
it." Another of the young women had, when in high
school, petitioned to play on the boys' tennis team in
Michigan. "I did it," she informed the *Globe*, "because I
wanted to play tennis, not because I wanted to be the first
woman breaking this barrier." Similar motivation, we are
told, led her to apply for a Rhodes. That same week, in
the *New York Times*, a woman orchestra conductor declared: "I have never felt discriminated against because
I was a woman. . . . I know that some orchestra managers,
when approached to engage me, have turned me down
because 'we already have hired our woman guest conductor for the season.' But it doesn't bother me."[6]

These were merely the latest in a long series of denials
of feminism that began long ago to interest me. Why, I
wondered, this compelling need to deny being a feminist, even on the part of those clearly intelligent enough
to see that without the feminists the Rhodes Scholarships
would not have been opened to women; women could
not have sued to play on boys' tennis teams; orchestras
could not have been persuaded to hire even one woman
conductor a season. No other group of people, anywhere, has ever felt impelled so persistently to deny their
association with those who have won for them the opportunities they now insist upon enjoying as their natural
and inevitable right.

Women writers have been little different. After inter-
viewing Margaret Drabble, Mel Gussow reports that her
most recent book "is a conscious effort on her part to
lose the label—undeserved—of 'woman's writer.' 'I was
fed up with women—slightly,' she said, explaining that

she wanted to write about a man as a central figure (similarly, she is tired of being asked to review books by other women)."[7] Drabble is not a unique example; I might have chosen many other writers. Her fear of being "ghettoized" into a world of "women's books" is not realistic. Being identified with other women and women writers at this time, however, threatens any woman: uncertain of her right to speak for all humanity regardless of sex, she is alternately compelled to encourage and repudiate other women.

Womanhood must be reinvented. Woman has too long been content to accept as fundamental the dependent condition of her sex. We avoid aggressive behavior, fear autonomy, feel incomplete without the social status only a man can bestow. In the past those women who have made their way successfully into the male-dominated worlds of business, the arts, or the professions have done so as honorary men, neither admiring nor bonding with other women, offering no encouragement to those who might come after them, preserving the socially required "femininity," but sacrificing their womanhood.

I do not here speak of those women whose deeds mark every period of feminist advance. The present feminist movement (already fading toward invisibility in the eyes of the young) produced many brave women of great accomplishment who never lost touch with their sense of themselves as women seeking freedom and autonomy in the opportunities opened up to them by their own movement. Yet we must understand that such women were helped to act because they drew strength from the movement as it gathered force in the 1960s and early 1970s. Excellent books tell us of the forces that allowed many women during those years to perceive the possibilities now open to them. But, looking beyond periods of what might be called "high feminism," I wish to examine those factors that enabled women who had no feminist or other group support to achieve, against all societal odds, a position of autonomy in male-dominated worlds. Although these women were, on the whole, remarkably unsupportive of other women, or unable to imagine other women as accomplished as themselves, they may provide a clue as to those qualities essential to female achievement.

In using myself as an example, I simply turn to what I know best in an attempt to understand the forces which operate upon a woman acting against the current of her times. I graduated from college into those post-World War II years when a return to the feminine mystique was universal, a shift inclusive even of the woman who was later to coin the phrase and name the process. I am not a behaviorist, and do not wish to discount inherent individual characteristics in myself or others. At the same time, I feel compelled to ask whether there may not be observable factors in my life and other lives that made such "unacceptable" behavior possible. No other woman in my high school graduating class, for example, immediately committed herself to a professional life.

What becomes evident in studying women like myself, women who moved against the current of their times, is that some condition in their lives insulated them from society's expectations and gave them a source of energy, even a sense of destiny, which would not permit them to accept the conventional female role. Some condition of being an outsider gave them the courage to be themselves.

Yet each of these outsiders, whatever she may teach us, failed to bring other women with her into the male world, failed to bond with women, failed to induce the male institutions she joined to accept members of her sex in significant numbers. The ideal condition of womanhood remained passivity. Activity or assertion, essential to achievement, induced in women capable of it a conflict between their assertiveness and the old ideal of womanhood: this conflict led, inevitably, to anxiety. Women, like all human beings, fear anxiety, and retreat before it; women of achievement choose, therefore, not to make themselves examples to other women or to encourage a new period of feminism.

There will appear to be, at the heart of my book, an inherent contradiction. On the one hand I deplore the fact that women of achievement, outside the brief periods of high feminism, have become honorary men, have consented to be token women rather than women bonded with other women and supporting them. On the other hand, I find that those women who *did* have the courage, self-confidence, and autonomy to make their way in the male-dominated world did so by identifying themselves with male ideals and role models. I want to tell women that the male role model for autonomy and achievement is, indeed, the one they still must follow. But if women's best hope of accomplishment is to follow male examples, am I not encouraging the very thing that I deplore?

This contradiction cannot be reconciled in the preface, but the spirit of reconciliation can be suggested. Women have denied themselves as examples the only models of achievement history offers us. Those women who accepted male ideals of achievement could restrain their inevitable anxiety only by not identifying themselves, within male institutions, as women. Sensing within themselves, as girls, a longing for accomplishment, they have, at great cost, with great pain, become honorary men, adopting at the same time the general male attitude toward women.

What I will suggest is that women, while not denying to themselves the male lessons of achievement that almost all our literature and history can afford, recognize the importance of taking these examples to themselves *as women,* supporting other women, identifying with them, and imagining the achievement of women generally. I want, therefore, to examine not only how, outside of the brief periods of high feminism, women have achieved positions in male-dominated worlds against great odds, but also how, in the future, they might in larger numbers repeat these accomplishments without being co-opted as honorary members of a male club.

Central to this whole question is the family: its condition, its survival, its essential nature. At the heart of women's problems (to say nothing of men's) is the nuclear family, where the nurturing is done almost entirely by the mother, while the representative of the outer world, the only alternative to the nurturing female, is inevitably male. As Nancy Chodorow concisely puts it, Freud and his followers demonstrated how this family works "with boys appropriating their masculine prerogatives and girls acquiescing in their feminine subordination and passivity."[8] This family structure, as I shall try to show, no longer successfully operates even for the fulfillment of its own aims. I believe that parenting must become the work of both sexes, and of more than a single individual, but I do not believe that Freud's essential insights about the development of the individual need therefore be sacrificed or abandoned.

Certainly conservatives voice a profound fear of the dissolution of the "family" and the loss of what they call traditional "moral values." At a deeper level, what they in fact fear, I think, is the necessity of living with change, with the risks and terrors and pain of reinvention. They have, of course, always retained an exceptional capacity for tolerating the pain of others. I mention conservatives because it is they who most often, and with the most publicity, speak as though the nuclear family that we all grew up in were the indispensable pillar of Western civilization, and women, in their passivity and submission, the irreplaceable foundation of the nuclear family. I do not believe this to be true; as Tocqueville put it:

> the more I study the former condition of the world and see the world of our own day in greater detail . . . the more I am tempted to believe that what we call necessary institutions are often no more than institutions to which we have grown accustomed, and that in matters of social constitution the field of possibilities is much more extensive than men living in their various societies are ready to imagine.[9]

Yet conservatives and reactionaries are not the major danger. The major danger lies in women's fear: the fear of being called inhuman. In the past, womanhood has served importantly to define manhood: boys and men defined themselves, from their first separation from the mother, as *not* feminine, *not* womanly. Men fear, perhaps, having nothing to define themselves against. Yet the rewards for them could be very great. Because of man's relation to his mother in the present family structure, men come to women looking for "narcissistic, phallic reassurance,"[10] not for intimacy, or companionship, or love. Both sexes, I believe, will gain enormously by ceasing to define themselves negatively against the other, by no longer striving to preserve every traditional difference.

Men have monopolized human experience, leaving women unable to imagine themselves as both ambitious and female. If I imagine myself (woman has always asked) whole, active, a self, will I not cease, in some profound way, to be a woman? The answer must be: imagine, and the old idea of womanhood be damned.

Today, as in the wake of all periods of high feminism, women are tempted to forsake the imagination of wholeness, almost before they have begun to embrace it. Woman is again reminding herself of what she has been told through the ages, at least through all recorded history: keep ambition and womanhood separate, do not let them near one another. (Some women are saying: combine your ambition and womanhood, but separate yourself from men.) Let us imagine ourselves as selves, as at once striving and female. Womanhood can be what we say it is, not what they have always said it was.

We must imagine ourselves accomplished; then we must imagine our accomplishments for other women, we must imagine other women equally with men as our companions, our friends, our peers. Literature is both the fruit and the nourishment of the imagination. We must look to it not only for the articulation of female despair and constriction, but also for the proclamation of the possibilities of life. We must ask women writers to give us, finally, female characters who are complex, whole, and independent—fully human.

In the essay that follows, I shall move on a winding path between life and literature, refusing to separate them, to confine myself, as a woman, to one or the other. Women have too long imagined only a constricted destiny for themselves, allowing the imagination of possibility to be appropriated for the exclusive use of men. It is time for women to claim an equal share in the ambitions as well as the frustrations of life.

Yes, womanhood must be reinvented. The materials for its reconstruction lie around us, some recovered or reinterpreted from the past, others revealed to us by students of our own time and place. In this book, I shall turn over many pieces and test many connections in the hope, finally, of assembling a possible new definition.

When I was a girl, my father told me the story of the bumble bee. According to the science of aeronautics, so the story went, it was impossible for a creature of the size and weight and construction of a bumble bee to fly. But the bumble bee, not having been told this, flies anyway.

2

Woman as Outsider

What is an outsider? An outsider, the *Oxford English Dictionary* tells us, is someone uninitiated into a body having special knowledge and power. Dickens dismissed a character in *Bleak House* as only an outsider and "not in the mysteries." Women are often outsiders twice over. The Jew, for example, has often been cited as the classic example of the outsider. Yet Jewish women were traditionally excluded from much of the religious observance by which Orthodox Jews marked their own identity.

At the simplest, most fundamental level, an outsider is

identified by exclusion from the cultural patterns of bonding at the heart of society, at its centers of power. Outsiders, however, may gain strength in their reaction to exclusion if they bond among themselves, offering each other comradeship, encouragement, protection, support. Again, one could cite the Jews as a remarkable case in point. Or, little as I care for analogies drawn from the animal kingdom, there is the inevitable example of Lionel Tiger's bachelor baboons. Excluded from the association of dominant males, females, and young, these subadult baboons form "all male groups," which Tiger calls peripheral. "The members of these groups may display considerable loyalty to each other," and roam together as a pack.[1]

Have women as outsiders also found strength in bonding? Smith-Rosenberg writes of the networks and friendships of women in the nineteenth century,[2] and these bonds seem very loving and supportive and free of all the pressures of psychoanalytic conservatism according to which any emotional attachment, genital or not, that women formed with other women, was pathological. Certainly the freedom of love and bonding, in the highly separate female and male spheres, was important, probably vital to the women's sanity.

Yet Smith-Rosenberg makes clear that such friendships and loves and networks were made possible by the sharply distinguished male and female worlds, and that these women not only accepted their special roles of domesticity and confinement to the family circle, they raised their daughters, with whom they seem to have had remarkably loving relationships, to take their place in this gentle, confined world. There was no thought of women collectively taking the initiative to alter it.[3]

In the modern period the woman's movement as a

whole and the myriad of small groups that make it up stand as attempts at female bonding. Yet women's position in society, or at least their traditional view of their position, puts them under social and psychological pressures that continually undermine their ability to bond. Women try to evade the psychological isolation of the outsider not by bonding with each other but rather by taking on the status of their husbands, if they are housewives, or by accepting the status of honorary male, if they succeed in penetrating the professional or business world. If we talk to the token woman lawyer, doctor, board member, tenured professor, we soon discover that she conceives herself not as an outsider but rather as an insider among men. No female bonding has so much as presented itself to her as a possibility. While an artist like Rosa Bonheur or a medical pioneer like Dr. Alice Hamilton may ask for professional identification for themselves, they will still insist upon the maternal destiny for other women. As I shall argue below, one does not apparently awaken to the awareness of being a female outsider, unless the condition of "outsiderness" has, through other means, entered one's consciousness.

Virginia Woolf long ago recognized that one major function of the woman's movement might be to organize women as self-conscious outsiders. She called for a Society of Outsiders, clearly defined, bonded, and outside of the major action. Although anonymous and elastic, as unlike male groups as possible, Woolf's Society of Outsiders would bind itself to certain aims, such as the refusal to support war, and the necessity of its members being paid for all duties performed, inside the home or out. These women would commit themselves primarily to independence and mutual support.[4] Woolf recognized that women have always been outsiders. She urged them to bond with one another on feminist principles. Woolf saw the necessary connection between bonding and becoming a force within society; but she also recognized that woman's indispensable first task is to *recognize* herself as outsider. For so close has woman been bonded to man—husband, father, mentor—that she has failed to see herself as having any status as insider or outsider beyond his. As current novels like French's *The Women's Room* well demonstrate, women in the suburbs may meet with one another to provide assorted comforts and rewards, but in these gatherings their relations with their husbands are rarely discussed in an intimate way. Such women commingle, but do not bond.

Outsider though she may be, woman does not think of herself as such, but takes her identity from her man: she is as far "in" or "out" as he. Joyce's *Ulysses* provides, inadvertently to be sure, an interesting comparison between the man and the woman as outsider. Leopold Bloom, the hero of *Ulysses,* remains, after countless imitations particularly among Jewish American authors, the exemplar of the "outsider," the man who moves in no group, who bonds with no one. A Jew in Ireland, baptized as a Christian, mocked by men and observing women only at a distance, Bloom is excluded from all the evident male bondings of Dublin, including even those to which Stephen, the self-styled exile, consents to belong. It has been said that Bloom at the entrance to the library, moves safely between the Scylla of one group and the Charybdis of another, but such an escape is also the price of not belonging there. Odysseus himself early loses his shipmates and struggles home alone, save for the aid of a goddess. Telemachus also is strikingly alone; Athene appears to him in the guise of a friend, but he is friendless. The suitors, of course, are bonded. But notice

Penelope, alone in her endeavors to hold off the suitors, to preserve Odysseus's home for him. When, finally, she is restored to her rightful position, it is by the side of her husband and son. Nor has Penelope ever, as they have done, found even momentary companionship or encountered her peer. (Fitzgerald, in the notes to his translation of the *Odyssey,* speaks of Penelope and Odysseus as "the faithful woman and the versatile, brave man."[5] Faithful is what one is, when one's courage depends on one's relation to a master, not to one's peers.) Furthermore, though Athene appears to both Odysseus and Telemachus in the guise of a friend and companion, she appears to Penelope *in a dream* as a distant sister. What companion does Penelope have whose guise she might assume? Who is equal and lives nearby, and is trusted by Penelope in matters relating to her husband? Allied primarily to a man in a relationship that cannot be described as bonding, the woman is outsider, even in comparison to that outsider, Odysseus, or the victim of usurpers, Telemachus.

Bloom differs from that earlier wanderer not least in having no possible bonding mates awaiting him at home. That he has no son is emphasis of this deprivation; a daughter in no way suffices. There are perhaps eight Jews in Dublin, so Bloom is isolated; as Mr. Deasy has boasted: we never let them in. Bloom, androgynous in all things, is perhaps most so in the extent to which he shares this isolation with women. The Jew in America, outsider in many ways, bonds fiercely with other Jews. Bloom is not even certain if he should greet the other Jew he meets, the butcher.

Is Bloom more isolated than Molly? Significantly, the question is never asked. That Molly does not care for women, and sees herself, in fantasy, only in connection with men, was for years assumed to be so typical of women as to require no comment. There is never any suggestion that her feeling for Milly will approach Bloom's for Stephen. On the contrary, her sexual attraction to Stephen is great. The loneliest man in literature has a wife whose loneliness is not even noticed, least of all by herself.

Men, who perceive women as by their sides, supporting them in whatever degree of "in" or "out" they enjoy, have rarely if ever described women as outsiders. Generally speaking, outsiders are conceived of in a context of alternate or excluded cultures. The outsider is expected to have a culture of his or her own (Jewish in America, Irish in England) that women, as women, patently lack. One might, in this context, persuade oneself that women are not even outsiders, because they do not all "come" from any particular place or culture. If a woman is an outsider, it is supposed that she is so only by virtue of being Black, or Jewish, or foreign born, but not by virtue of being a woman.

That distressing attitude of achieving women: "I made it, why can't you," that failure to sympathize with the struggles of less vigorous female selves, has always marked successful women. They refuse to understand the tokenism that they represent, refuse to see that their single presence, far from proving that anyone can make it, determines, under the present system, that no one else will. In fact, a woman of accomplishment almost always feels a scorn for other women that, although rarely chronicled, goes far to explain the failure of female bonding among women who have entered the male sphere.

What happens here—and I shall discuss this subsequently—is that the woman no longer, if she ever did, sees herself as belonging to the same species as other women. She has become an honorary male, she is a member of their club, she is more royalist than the king. Thus a *woman* Jungian explains the feminine: "When *we* ask about the feminine, we talk about our concepts of the human person and of relationships between persons. We touch the most intimate aspects of our lives—our relations to sexuality, to *our wives,* our daughters, our mothers, to feminine elements in the male personality, and to the unconscious."[6]

The despising of females is particularly notable in those exceptional Victorian women who broke through some of the severest strictures against women. Caroline Norton, after her great struggle with the marriage laws culminating in the Married Woman's Property Act, had no sympathy with the woman's movement and made fun of the women in it.[7] In 1889 there appeared a protest against woman's suffrage signed by Mrs. Humphrey Ward and Beatrice Webb: "We believe the emancipating process has now reached the limits fixed by the physical constitution of women."[8] (At the same time, we might notice, Sidney Webb and Bernard Shaw were in favor of the woman's movement.) Florence Nightingale, whose struggle for a meaningful life is one of the most moving in recorded history, had an active dislike for feminist writing and propaganda. She wrote to Harriet Martineau to say "I am brutally indifferent to the rights and wrongs of my sex." To another woman she wrote of her wide experience of women all over the world. "Yet I leave no school behind me. My doctrines have taken no hold among women. Not one of my Crimean following learnt anything from me, or gave herself for one moment after she came home to carry out the lesson of that war or of those hospitals."[9]

Françoise Giroud, France's first woman cabinet member, responded to the question "Were you a feminist?" thus: "No, not at all. Girls bored me, I found them dull and tiresome, with their endless stories. . . . I was the traitor, the one who had gone over to the men's camp." Asked about one of the women editors with whom she had first worked, Giroud said that she had had a "kind of love" for her, but not friendship. "I think," she explained, "I can honestly say that I know what friendship is and means; it's something I practice with men, carefully and meticulously."

Giroud surmised of her editor, the very successful Helene Lazareff, that "in her heart of hearts," she never "believed that women have" any other function in life except to seduce men. . . . "To hold a man, or several men, was for her the epitome of female gamesmanship."

Similarly, accomplished women like Jane Addams, the founder of Hull House, Rosa Bonheur, Frances Perkins, FDR's Secretary of Labor—to take women from three professions—however much they may have found fulfillment in professional activity, were always assuring other women that their true destiny lay in their relationship to men, whether in wifehood, motherhood, or in the home. From political platforms, Phyllis Schlafly, leader of the anti-Equal Rights Amendment and anti-abortion movement, has done the same thing, as did Marynia Farnham and other women psychoanalysts from behind their professional desks. In every case, the generality of women are seen as radically, and it would appear, irremediably different from "me."

What I have called the "despising of females" manifests itself ubiquitously and most poignantly in the woman's wish for a male child. Adrienne Rich, the poet and author of *Of Woman Born,* has recognized this passion, as it is almost always recognized, in retrospect:

When I first became pregnant I set my heart on a son. (In our childish, "acting-out" games I had always preferred the masculine roles and persuaded or forced my younger sister to act the feminine ones.) I still identified more with men than with women; the men I knew seemed less held back by self-doubt and ambivalence, more choices seemed open to them. I wanted to give birth, at twenty-five, to my unborn self . . . someone independent, actively willing, original.[10]

Rich observes that the woman's son is the masculine part of her, played out in the only acceptable way, and quotes the words of Ruth Benedict, before she knew she could not have children, before she became a renowned anthropologist:

Does this sense of personal worth, this enthusiasm for one's own personality belong only to great expressive souls? or to a mature period of life I have not yet attained? or may I perhaps be shut off from it by eternal law because I am a woman, and lonely? It seems to me the one priceless gift of this life:—of all blessings on earth I would choose to have a man child who possessed it.[11]

The belief, clearly enough, is that true enthusiasm is so nonpassive a gift, that it must belong, properly, in a male body. Rather than watch their daughters suffer with such enthusiasm, or live without it, women long for sons. Even Mary Wollstonecraft, as Rich reports, watching the passivity in the women around her, had been "led to imagine that the few extraordinary women who have rushed in eccentrical directions out of the orbit prescribed to their sex, were *male* spirits, confined by mistake in female frames."[12]

There is strong evidence, in short, that accomplished women in male-dominated professions are, as the phrase goes, male-identified. Freud and especially his followers have perhaps irremediably damaged that phrase, leaving one with the sense of a sexually disoriented woman, of someone with gender confusion. Nothing could be further from the truth. These women accept allegiance with the males of whose group they are a part, even while themselves wholly female in their sexuality and gender identity.

Women in the world of events, whether they be prime ministers, women psychoanalysts, Cabinet members, or otherwise members of a dominantly male profession, have bonded with the male world they have joined, and have failed to envision other women at their side. Needless to say, they have not found them there.

In December, 1971, the tenured women in the Graduate Faculties of Arts and Sciences at Columbia University met together for the first time. Not only had these women never met before as a group, they had never thought of themselves as a group. It may be stated with certainty that the idea of such a gathering had never entered one of their minds. Tenured faculty members of either sex regarded themselves, without question, as members of particular departments. No other loyalty so much as suggested itself, apart from a general sense of allegiance to the University as a whole, a sense strengthened by the recent student uprisings, particularly among the more conservative members, devoted as they were to a university whose old-fashioned sense of itself was rapidly receding from possibility.

The idea of meeting was mine; the woman's movement had by then sufficiently caught me up—not in its beliefs, which I had shared, it seemed to me, from birth, but in its sense of the possibility of action. My colleague Joan Ferrante and I, having been informed by the university administration that they had no idea of the number of women on its faculty (this denial of data was the first of many, but probably the only honest one) had ourselves to discover the members of this new "group." We each knew a few tenured women, and a systematic search through the catalogue produced the names of the others. Some men with ambiguous names confused us, for a short time. In the end we had a group of fourteen women, out of a tenured faculty of approximately 325. All these women were in their forties or beyond, except one, who was the youngest by at least ten years. We did not call upon the women professors of Barnard (the woman's undergraduate college of Columbia and a separate corporation), Teacher's College, the School of Social Work, or any of the professional schools, at that time. Included, however, were the faculties of Columbia College (no tenured women) and the School of General Studies, Columbia's adult undergraduate college, to which over the years, tenured women had tended to be relegated.

Although I was far from realizing it at the time, I had in that list of fourteen names powerful evidence of the forces that make possible the process of female achievement in male-dominated professions. What I also had was a collection of accomplished women, few of whom felt anything but discomfort, in some cases acute discomfort, at the thought of identifying themselves with a "woman's group," or, indeed, as women at all.

Let me repeat, once again, what I mean when I say that they did not identify themselves as women. I do *not* mean what Freud or any of his followers, professional or par-lor, would have meant. The "Freudian" view that accom-plished women are sexually men, or trying to be, has done more, I suspect, than any other misconception to doom women to fear of accomplishment and selfhood. No woman I have studied had, for any moment in her life, any doubt of her sexuality, her "core gender iden-tity," as it later came to be called.[13] When I say that these women identified themselves as men, I mean that, finding no role for themselves in the accepted position of housewife and mother, they joined the club of profes-sional men and became full-fledged members, suspi-cious of any diminution of that club's exalted standards.

That few of these fourteen women were willing to identify themselves with women, or openly to support other women in overcoming disqualifications and dis-criminations did not become evident until considerably later. Our first meeting was, in any case, not a conscious-ness-raising session in the sense that phrase would later come to convey. I do not think that any woman in that group had ever contemplated such a process. What we all most certainly felt, in gathering together, was aston-ishment.

Nothing of great consequence resulted from our first session and after one or two more tries we gave up the attempt to meet as a group. What the meetings did pro-vide me, however, was my first insight into the character and backgrounds of women likely to have reached pro-fessorial rank in a prestigious, male-dominated univer-sity before the current woman's movement was under-way. After my year at the Radcliffe Institute, and especially after a study of the work of Margaret Hennig, to which I shall return in a moment, I realized that the facts about these fourteen seemed to say a good deal about the woman as outsider—both as unconventional American girl and as a member of some group apart from the central culture.

With one exception, herself almost a member of what was to become a "feminist" generation, all these women were born between 1912 and 1929, and matured in the thirties and forties. No feminist force supported them in their ambitions and endeavors. They met as individuals, and as individuals they had arrived in the position so to meet, each on her own.

All but one of these fourteen women had what Patricia Albjerg Graham has called "close ties to another cultural heritage."[14] More than half of them had not been born in the United States, but had come to this country after early childhood, or later. Of the five who had been born in the United States, two had close family ties to a European heritage, and two were Jewish. Only one was a "typical" American, born in the western United States of parents who were themselves the children of Protestant forebears born on this continent.

At least eleven of the fourteen women came from all-girl families. Six were only children; the seventh had a brother eight years older. Six of those from all-girl families were the eldest.

The significance of these facts is illuminated by Margaret Hennig's work.[15] Hennig set out to study women in high managerial positions in the business world (an emphatically male domain) who had a continuous work history and held, at the time of investigation, a current position at a high level, without kinship ties to the ownership of the firm. The women chosen for the study were not in a position or business considered "feminine," such as the cosmetics industry.

Of the women Hennig studied *all* were first born, or

virtually in the situation of the first born, and came from an all-girl family. In other words, each of Hennig's women was in a position to be chosen by her father as "son," since no boy was present to fill that role. All of these women had extremely close relationships with their fathers, enjoyed with him excursions into "male" worlds, and were continually involved with him in activities conventionally described as "masculine." The father was the role model; the mother, while regarded with affection, was tolerated as "a mother" in a generalized way: the daughter had no intention of repeating her pattern of life. They did not have to accept the fact that, being girls, they "necessarily took second place in the order of things." They had, as children, a strong preference for adults, and a certain lack "of interaction with children their own age." The major struggle was to think of themselves as girls, yet successful and active. Although they developed so-called masculine attributes, they did not abandon definitions of themselves as female.

Like other women of achievement, they found they "didn't like women on general principles. That is, I didn't like to be with women. They made me feel very uncomfortable, but I also disapproved of them. I thought they were stupid and I always thought they felt the same about me!"[16]

The differences between the Hennig group and the Columbia group are perhaps worth noting. The Hennig women, born between 1910 and 1915, were more likely to have felt the breezes, if not the winds, of an earlier feminist movement. They were all, in addition, born in the United States of upwardly aspiring middle-class families. None of the Hennig women married until past her middle thirties, and none had children, though some did acquire stepchildren. Of the Columbia women, ten were married, and most of these had children. That difference reflects, I think, the differing patterns of professional success in the business and the academic world. In the business world, Hennig's women all rose with the aid of a mentor: some man in a position sufficiently powerful to promote the interests of the woman manager had helped her individually in her rise. The necessity of the woman's devoting all her time and attention to her work, and to that mentor, precluded marriage.

In the academic world, I believe, there is typically no such close relationship of mentor and woman follower. (I preclude the woman who becomes the mistress of a professor who then promotes her career; such things happen, but not in any of these cases.) The demands of the academic life, while exigent, are so in a different way. Although I have discussed none of this with any of the women concerned, I believe that marriage and motherhood permitted academic women at that time (spanning the postwar marriage and baby boom) to feel more comfortable with their unusual accomplishments and status in the academic world. Perhaps equally important, the flexible daily schedule of academic work more easily accommodated family life. As one of the fourteen women who married and had children, I must be suspected, of course, simply of projecting what I now recognize as my own past needs upon the histories of these other women.

It seems evident, from the statistics available to me about the Columbia women, that a foreign background frequently provided the impetus toward achievement in America, even if the American culture did not then endorse such achievement for girls. The importance of the father to the child's life, an importance made possible by the lack of male children in the family, may be a common factor in the Columbia group, as it surely is in Hennig's sample. Since I have spoken about their lives with only two of the Columbia women, and these two are, after all, friends, I cannot be certain what role fathers played in the lives of the others. However, in the case of the two American-born Columbia women who were Jews, their fathers certainly served as role models.

I was one of the American-born Jewish women; to me, my father was the only possible role model. I had in common with Hennig's women the emotional support of my mother in the struggle toward autonomy, although her life, like that of women generally, seemed to me utterly beyond contemplation as a possible destiny for me. I realize now that I never really wanted to know about my father's childhood, just as he never wished, until after my mother's death, to talk about it, because it was something we both conceived of as past, overcome, left behind. That we knew, intellectually, the impossibility of this is, of course, beside the point. Yet what operated for us both, I now see, was a sense of being able to change life *now*. Adrienne Rich, many years later, formulated this conviction for us:

> If I cling to circumstances I could feel
> not responsible. Only she who says
> she did not choose, is the loser in the end.

My mother never ceased blaming circumstances for her life. Of course, she was right: women were left with little choice. Eventually they must learn to choose, as male children choose. As I understand my father had chosen.

I never knew my father's family. The strangeness of this did not occur to me until many years later. My father, in fact, deliberately chose to separate me from the conditions and influences from which he had already separated himself. Can I convey his sense of the ignorance and superstition that surrounded him in childhood? When his father died in Russia, my father, a child of four with a grieving mother, was continually asked by the village women: "What have you done to your father?" He wished to give me, and provide for himself, distance from the crudity and despair of such beginnings. He supported his mother all her life, as well as his youngest sister when she required help.

His two oldest sisters required no help, then or later. When Fanny was fourteen and Mollie twelve, they had come alone to this country to earn the passage money for their mother, their younger sister Mary, and the baby, my father. I have never been able to grasp what that task required of them in the way of courage and determination. They earned money sewing for the Manhattan Shirt Company, starting each at the wage of $2.50 a week. From this they saved enough for tickets to be sent back to Russia. Fanny and Mollie supported the family until my father took over that responsibility when he was fourteen.

When my father underwent an operation later in life, he asked me to be sure to "take care of Fanny," though I had never met her. She was the last of his sisters to survive, though the oldest. His gratitude to her, for making his life in America possible, never abated.

When my mother agreed to marry my father—he was utterly in love, I suspect both with her and her mother —it was, as she often told me, against the advice of her doctor cousin, who said my father's mother was crazy. Probably his mother was depressed and lonely, as well as careless of her appearance. She spoke only Yiddish, and loved her son above all else. Out of some sense of self-preservation, he broke that emotional bond early. At seventeen he had a mustache (which he has kept all his life) and he called himself twenty-one, to get a job requiring that age; thereafter he was legally four years older than his actual age. He waited until the correct actual age to begin to collect social security, and only straightened the matter out very late in life, after my mother had died.

Mary, his youngest sister, had clearly been very bright, as he was, and her teacher had come to the home one day to try to persuade the mother not to permit the child to leave school and go to work. She climbed the stairs to a small, attic apartment to find a mother who could not speak English and a boy of ten. My father always remembered the look in her eyes as she took in the hopelessness of the situation. After a few minutes, she retreated. I think that lost opportunity haunted my father and may explain in some part the complete support he always offered me in any professional or educational pursuit.

My father himself suffered in school as a child, whether because he was Jewish or for other reasons is not clear. As a very small boy, perhaps in Europe (this I heard from my mother) he had been sent to board at a school run by a rabbi. He was starved and lonely. The experience filled him with disdain for institutionalized religions, including Judaism, which never really left him, though it became less emotion-laden in later years. Schooling was another matter. In America and in public school, aged about six, he rapidly learned English and earned money teaching it to older men. He was brilliant at mathematics always, and one teacher corrected the other students' papers simply by comparing them to his. Once he made a mistake and she was furious with him. He learned from that the unforgivable: to fail expectations, however unreasonable.

Twice he was put back by a sadistic principal for reasons of discipline. The first time he repeated the term, sitting through the classes, and he made up the missed term in the summer. The second time he was disciplined for not staying perfectly in line while marching down the hall. Desperate, knowing he could not go on, he went up to consult a teacher who had encouraged him. "Wait here," she said. When she returned, an hour later, she assured my father that it would be all right. Years later my father looked her up, to express his recognition of her as the person who had saved him, and she remembered the incident well: she knew the principal to be a heavy drinker, and she had threatened him with exposure if he did not rescind the order. My father has said that that defeat would have broken him utterly; the occasional helping hand made his life possible.

At seventeen, he left home. He worked full time, taught himself to be an expert typist and shorthand taker, for which he won a medal in a contest sponsored by a typewriter company, put himself through college at night, and became a certified public accountant. By the time he was thirty, when I was born, he had become a partner in a brokerage firm and made a million dollars. He and my mother were surprised when she discovered herself to be pregnant; my mother, the oldest of seven, had not planned to have children.

My mother's family, Austrians, were, according to some mysterious class standard always unintelligible to an outsider, at a very much higher range of being than my father's family. For one thing, my mother, the oldest, had been born in the United States. For another her parents, married in America, had always lived together, somewhat too much so. Years later, when my mother

asked her mother why she had had so many children, my
grandmother said: "I didn't know any better." For years
she and my grandfather slept on different floors, perhaps
their attempt at birth control. My mother was seventeen
when the youngest was born, and she was terribly
ashamed.

My grandmother, one of Howe's sustaining women,
not only ruled the household with an arm of iron, but
kept a store to support them all, her blond, blue-eyed
husband enjoying life rather than struggling through it.
My grandmother was one of those powerful women who
know that they stand between their families and an outside world filled with temptations to failure and shame.
I remember her as thoroughly loving. But there can be
no question that she impaired her six daughters for autonomy as thoroughly as if she had crippled them—more
so. The way to security was marriage; the dread that
stood in the way of this was sexual dalliance, above all
pregnancy. The horror of pregnancy in an unmarried
girl is difficult, perhaps, to recapture now. For a Jewish
girl not to be a virgin on marriage was failure. The male's
rights were embodied in her lack of sexual experience,
in the knowledge that he was the first, the owner.

All attempts at autonomy had to be frustrated. And of
course, my grandmother's greatest weapon was her own
vulnerability. She had worked hard, only her daughters
knew how hard. She could not be comforted or repaid—
as *my* mother would feel repaid—by a daughter's accomplishments, only by her marriage.

What sustained my grandmother, apart from her
hopes for her children, was the Jewish religion. She
donated some of her scarce funds to the homeland; she
kept a kosher home. My grandmother welcomed her Jewish relatives, whose manners and faith appalled my

mother even as a small child. All about her, the gentile children seemed gayer, happier, less burdened with guilt and fear. Blond like them, she wanted to be one of them. Christmas seemed to her a time of joy like nothing she had ever experienced; in those days, merchants had not yet commercialized its Jewish counterpart, Hanukkah.

From an early age, therefore, my mother identified all that limited her life as Judaism. She wanted desperately to work, was accepted for training as a nurse, but her mother wept that she would be ruined. My mother had never finished high school, a fact of which she was deeply ashamed, because she could not understand arithmetic, and had no one to ask about it. So she went off to secretarial school, becoming a skilled stenographer, but worked only until she was married at twenty-three. During my childhood and adolescence she had few responsibilities—there was only one child, my mother "entertained" rarely, and we always had "help." Yet the less she had to do, the less she did. I was left largely to care for myself (no doubt useful training in self-reliance). Even now, I cannot think of the emptiness and futility of my mother's life without pain.

In her adolescence my mother sent away for books on religion, what was then called "New Thought." She was searching for something beyond the dogmatic beliefs of her family. She got a job in a bank that did not hire Jews, following the advice of her secretarial school teacher that she should not tell them she was Jewish, since she did not look it, and her name was anomalous. She determined then and there to cut herself off from everything Jewish and "common," her favorite word of condemnation. She urged my father to change his name, but he would not do this. Through all his life his clients were gentile and knew him to be Jewish. For that reason he would never work on the High Holy days.

My mother's horror of everything Jewish was never mitigated, though Hitler prevented her from finally passing out of the Jewish scene altogether. Even for her, that became impossible. But to the very end, if we saw Hassidic Jews on the streets of New York, she would insist on analyzing for me how horrible they looked, how utterly unattractive were their clothes and manners.

My mother was the only member of her family who did not continue to practice Judaism, though her sisters and brother moved away from the Orthodox tradition in which they had been raised. As long as my grandmother lived, her children (even my mother) would prepare kosher food for her when she visited. I used to spend much time with my grandmother, who was for me the chief loving force in my early childhood. When I was a baby, my mother gave her, during one of my long stays there, the doctor's suggested diet for me. It contained bacon. My mother had assumed that the bacon would be ignored. Instead, my grandmother got a special pan, and burner, and cooked it for me in the cellar.

Just before the depression, in 1928, the head of my father's firm was struck down, though not killed, by a heart attack. My father then suffered a nervous breakdown. Unable to function, and with numerous physical ailments, he was finally advised to undergo psychoanalysis. It was a last resort, undertaken with little hope, but after two and a quarter years of sessions five days a week, he was cured. It has often occurred to me that my father more closely resembled Freud's early patients with their well-marked neurotic symptoms than those patients of our own time whose symptoms are less physical, more in the nature of deep dissatisfactions with life. Under analysis, he recognized that his guilt at his father's death, reinforced by the ignorant community of his childhood, was reenacted in the heart attack of his head partner. His psychoanalysis left him with a lasting admiration for Freud and a deep interest in those religions that understood the effects of the mind upon the body.

My father's brokerage position and wealth disappeared in the depression. Left with no money or job, he returned to the profession of C.P.A. In 1932, he borrowed on his very large insurance policy (all that was left to him of his former wealth) and moved, with my mother and me, to New York City. It was a new start. In time, he remade his fortune but, unlike the typical American businessman of that time, once he had made the amount he aimed for, he quit.

For my mother, the depression was, in some sense, the last event in her life. She never recovered the confidence, tenuous at best, that financial success had offered her. She could not bring herself to spend money. Years later, when she lived on Fifth Avenue, she would walk long blocks east to the A & P to save small sums. She saw independence for a woman as money in the bank, and out of the generous allowances my father gave her, she saved her money. When she died quite suddenly, that fair sum came to me. Alas, it was as much evidence of her fear as of her love.

In 1936, on my mother's fortieth birthday, her mother was hit by a car and died several hours later. I was ten years old, and evaded, through that accident, not only any future imperfections I might later have found in my grandmother, that complete figure of love, but also any influence toward Judaism. My grief, and my mother's, was terrible. For years I dreamed of my grandmother, as did my mother.

I was sent to a private school where, although many of

the students were Jewish, the tone was distinctly high
Episcopalian. My favorite days in the year were the Jewish holidays when I, and the gentile children, were in
school, the student body much diminished in number.
Had I been offered three wishes, one of them, I now
guess, would have been not to be Jewish. Like my
mother, I enjoyed the gentile ambience, and interpreted
the gospels in my own way.

I was not without religious instruction. Sometime in
the thirties my parents began attending the "Divine Science" Church of the Healing Christ every Sunday, and
took me with them. At first it met in some enormous hall
on Thirty-fourth Street, then in the Hippodrome, finally
in Carnegie Hall. It was essentially a popular version of
the "Ancient Wisdom," probably not too far from the
religious movements of today that incorporate Eastern
religious elements. The pastor, Emmet Fox, a man of
extraordinary power, published his books with Harper's;
many of them are still in print, though Fox died over
twenty years ago. Each Sunday he read a passage from
the New Testament, we sang Protestant hymns (often
with the verses changed to be more positive, less Calvin-
ist in tone), and Fox would deliver a sermon taking off
from the passage. Looking back now, I find the whole
thing in many ways too Emersonian, too consoling. Even
as a child, I guessed there was something not quite
"right" about it, and told no one of "my" church—but
not, I think, because it was not a Jewish one. Yet it must
be said in fairness that Fox and his "higher thought" did
much to sustain me in an anxious childhood. I com-
municated with him only once, upon my application to
college. I wrote to ask him whether or not I should tell
Wellesley and Smith (the only two colleges to which I
applied) that I was Jewish, when in fact I did not believe

in the religion. He wrote back that he thought I should tell them, and I did. Both accepted me.

Being an outsider as a Jew made me somehow better able to bear, or to accept as inevitable, my status as outsider because I was female. Whether, had I been the victim of egregious anti-Semitism, I would have reacted in a similar way, I do not know. I suspect not. It was as a secret outsider that I operated, as Jew, as female. I pretended to be a part of two worlds, the gentile, the male, to neither of which I belonged.

Malcolm Cowley has mentioned, in *Exile's Return*, the anomaly of Jewish kids from a tradition of immigration, labor struggles, and street gangs who write, not of those things, but of English abbeys they have never seen and nightingales they have never heard. All this has changed, so that when reading American Jewish fiction today, one longs occasionally for a nightingale. But even at the time, I used to wonder, did Cowley understand the literary impulse behind all those Keatsian endeavors? Perhaps it was mainly imitative and snobbish: not only did this seem to be "real" poetry, but clearly it was the "literary," "gentlemanly" way of life. No doubt my mother and I were unduly attracted to it, but it seemed so refreshing a change from the worrying, self-pitying passion of the Jews. It would be many years—for not even the Wellesley experience taught me this truth—until I discovered the essential deadness at the heart of "proper" Anglo-Saxon demeanor. Sometime in the sixties the word WASP became, for perhaps the first time in history, a pejorative word, and as I came to understand its coldness I stood amazed, as before a great revelation.

In some way, my mother knew this. She had a word "goyish" which she used, very much *en famille*, for everything tasteless, in the sense of without savor, without gusto, in life. She particularly applied this word to food: peas and creamed chicken, salad with cut-up celery in it, but in fact she meant anything washed out or lacking in vigor. She admired Gertrude Stein long before that became fashionable, mostly because she "led her own life," partly because, although Jewish, Stein had repudiated what my mother called "all that Jewish nonsense," and partly, I think, because Stein was vigorous and warm, not a WASP.

In some sense, those young Jewish poets of whom Cowley spoke were rootless and seemed, in their longing for quiet, discretion, and an orderly world, to have found the roots they would have chosen, given a choice, in the Anglican tradition. Maurice Schwartz in his book *The Gentleman and the Jew* did, indeed, contrast the two traditions, but in favor of the Jewish. I read the book and was left amazed that there was any question open: the gentleman, the Greek was clearly the more desirable alternative. Did I, even then, guess that the Greek, the gentlemanly, English tradition, at least allowed for the possibility of bringing women into the mainstream of the culture?

The connection between Jewishness, feminism, and rootlessness is worth pursuing. My mother was not alone in her break away from Jewishness, her sense that Jewishness was exactly what held the Jewish mother confined in her "sustaining" role. I am certain that it was my grandmother's orthodoxy, her acceptance of her role as server, that, in my mother's eyes, imprisoned her and her daughters. In *Ulysses* only Leopold Bloom is cosmopolitan as opposed to rooted, and Bloom's androgynous or womanly nature is not unconnected with this.

For a short time after college, I was given the chance to learn about Conservative Judaism at first hand. I was offered a job at the Jewish Theological Seminary as the coordinator of a radio program they were producing. Since it reflects more upon me than upon them, I readily admit that I found both the rabbis and the rabbinical students in that institution highly distasteful. I hated them and myself for hating them, equally. Two pivotal occasions, both having to do with the elevator, will illustrate my problem. I and one of the young rabbis one day waited for the elevator, which was self-service. It arrived: at that moment, if someone did not open the outer door of the elevator, it would leave. I, a well-brought up young lady, waited for the man to open the door. He, a Conservative Jew, waited for the woman to open it. The elevator departed. On another occasion, in the elevator, one rabbi told another that the president of the Seminary had just had a granddaughter. "What did they name her?" he was asked. "Who thinks of names for girls?" he shrugged. I handed in my resignation that afternoon.

A high administrator who liked my work asked me why I was leaving. Although I was not a practicing Jew, he hoped to keep me in the fold. Perhaps he liked the tone he thought I added; the work I did was chiefly with non-Jewish people and institutions. I decided to be frank with him and told him the story about the granddaughter's name. There followed from him a long explanation about the different roles the Jews had for men and women. True, women could perform none of the religious functions; their job at home was too important for them to waste their time on that. But they were honored equally with men.

I knew this not to be true, and I think he knew it. Indeed, he told me more than he intended. I discovered that to a Jew women are, in fact, seen as vile—there is no other word. I asked a secretary for the rules for keeping a Jewish home and studied them. The horror with which a Jewish woman was to respond to a vaginal discharge from her body exceeded even my expectations. I resigned not only from the Seminary, but from the Jewish religion. As the least feminist of beliefs, excepting only the Moslem, Judaism had handed me the excuse I needed.[17]

The religion from which I did not resign was that "Ageless Wisdom" in which my father believed. Perhaps the most important aspect of this which he passed on to me was his conviction of the efficacy of will and destiny. You could do what you set yourself to do. More than that, in that secret part of the self where faith resides, he was convinced that there was a pattern to the world. Somewhere those, more evolved and wiser, watched and helped us; inevitably one's goodness was somewhere understood and noticed. He would not, for he is a highly intelligent man, have put his faith that naively, but so it came through to me. The idea, therefore, that I was destined to accomplish "something" was never far from me. Certainly this idea carried greater weight than the world's opinion that women were expected to accomplish nothing in the wider sphere.

None of the other fourteen tenured women at Columbia in 1971, it is safe to guess, had enacted a life resembling mine; the very idea might shock and disturb them. For one thing, I have the sense, that their origins were socially "higher" than mine, that they would never have thought of themselves as "scraped off the Lower East Side," and certainly they would not have thought so with pride, as I do. My Gatsby sense of self-creation, acquired from my father, is not, as far as I know, shared by any of them.

They resemble me, however, in being separate, clearly

distinguishable from their cohort or generation. For most of them, foreign birth alone proclaims that distinction. It never occurred to one of them that she was not "somebody." Perhaps I was also alone in rejecting, in my mother, the ideas of gentility and impeccable taste as the assurance of status. I have a sense that my mother's terrible failure, as I saw it, and more importantly, as she saw it, helped to make me more feminist than most other women of my generation.

It has only been in recent years, since my mother's death, that I have been able to understand her suffering or, more exactly, as I have learned from the work of the theologian Dorothee Soelle, her failure to experience suffering. My mother's life, and the lives of all those mothers whose destinies seemed to their daughters impossibly confined, can, I now believe, be seen with particular clarity in the light of Soelle's work on suffering. There are two forms of suffering, the first with the passivity of quiet endurance, the second, as a form of change, a mode of becoming.[18] Soelle has said that "the more a person perceives his suffering as a natural part of life, the lower his self esteem. . . . To be caught up in one role, without flexibility, predisposes one to suffer."[19] Women have, on the whole, been unable to see the possibility of change in their suffering, often to the point of not even being able, or willing, to articulate their pain. This is because their role in life, as nurturer, supporter, helpmate seemed ordained, and therefore impossible to transform. Indeed, such a transformation might appear to challenge the divine order, if one saw the acceptance of one's lot as religious submission. Such a view is what Soelle calls Christian (one might add, Jewish) masochism.

In addition to this, the woman as sufferer, where she

is not part of a generally debased population (as in poverty or war—though here, she will always be more debased than her male counterparts, more used, more humiliated), will, even in desolate bitterness, see within her destiny the possibility of loving. If she deserts a brutal husband, can she as well desert her children? And if the husband is not brutal, but simply without imagination as to her need for change or for a destiny of her own, still, in convincing herself that she loves, she convinces herself that her own suffering is of secondary importance. Further, if a person perceives herself as chosen by another human being, a man, she is thereby disabled from seeing herself as chosen by destiny, by the process of becoming. Men, in choosing women to marry, provide them with a destiny. Women, even if they choose the men (as Elizabeth Bennet in Jane Austen's *Pride and Prejudice* "chose" Darcy), choose only to be chosen. From then on, any change will be not sought but thrust upon them. This state, if not slavery, is not freedom.

Soelle has set forth what she calls the three phases of suffering. Although she did not deal specifically with the situation of women, I think her model accurately describes their mental states. Let me suggest how it might apply. Phase one is mute, speechless suffering, marked by isolation, domination by the situation, and the inability to organize objectives. The sufferer in this phase sees her proper action as submissiveness and powerlessness. Most women throughout the world, even if they are not abject victims of poverty or violence, live in this phase, tending, if any perception is allowed them, toward a sensation of meaninglessness.

Phase two is the state of articulation. This phase is achieved by women only rarely, and then only in highly industrialized countries, though in larger numbers during periods of feminism. In phase two the sufferer becomes aware, and able to speak, to express her despair, to communicate. She is able to analyze the situation in which she suffers. Clearly, this phase is equivalent, in a period of feminism, to the consciousness-raising groups, the development of interchange, the breaching of isolation. The third phase, the one reached by more than individual and scattered women only in a period of high feminism, is that in which actual change is accomplished: it is marked by solidarity of the sufferers, by common recognition of and agreement about objectives, and by organizing to reach them through the conquest of powerlessness.

Probably women are the only large group of the oppressed who over the centuries have remained in phase one. They do so both for the reasons mentioned, and also because so many of them, whether on account of male identification or misguided notions of submission, have successfully avoided articulation, have not even conceived change. Unlike other slaves and oppressed people, they have rarely, in Western countries, been in the desperate position of having nothing to lose. Articulation and change would both necessitate risking objects of their love and perhaps the state of being depended upon, of being needed. Women have tended not to recognize the pain inherent in lack of selfhood, or, if they recognize it to the extent of responding with general depression and despair, they have been unable to articulate it.[20] It is important to realize that the crucial phase for the majority of women is not three, but two, and it is here that women have notoriously failed: they have not been able to articulate their pain except in periods of feminism, and then often with little solidarity and much opposition from other women.

Why do women resist recognizing their own suffering or feel guilty if they do perceive it and fail to articulate it? Soelle would say that they exist in a state of apathy, protected from the realization of suffering, and the experience of pain. To perceive their own suffering would be to open them to other suffering, to rob them of the protection they have carefully built up against the experience of pain. Women have avoided adventure, risk, and opportunity because they have been taught that suffering, the shaking loose of the comfortable foundations of one's life, must be avoided at all costs.

If I look back on my mother's life, at least in the years when I shared it, I can see it as entirely organized to avoid suffering, her own or others'. The degree to which she managed to insulate herself against the pain in the world was extraordinary. But she insulated herself against more than that: against any damage to her furniture, by rarely inviting guests to her house; against the possibility of failure, by following no endeavor past the first enthusiasms; against the loss of money, though she could well have spared it; and against trust, for it would probably be betrayed.

I remember her despair, her depression, more vividly than any experience in my life, certainly I felt it more palpably than anything else in my childhood. Yet articulation was beyond her. She knew that she ought to be doing something, working at something, but her fear of being taken advantage of, of perhaps having to fight, to be sneered at, to fail, was too great. And then, it might be revealed that she had never finished high school. By the time I discovered this last fear, and tried to persuade her that it was no longer an insurmountable obstacle, and certainly not a matter of shame, it was far too late.

Yet, to anyone seeing her, she seemed the most fortunate of women. Certainly she must have seemed so to many people in the depression, to her sisters, to my grandmother. She was beautiful, rich, lived elegantly, attended lectures and museums, had a husband who was utterly devoted (in his way), and a child. Three times before the war she went off to Europe on a cruise. My father refused to travel; I now suppose because the trauma of the original migration was still before him, or possibly because he did not want to apply for a passport and have the date of his birth investigated (though that is only supposition). I was sent to camp from a very early age, six I think, and one year my mother was in Europe and did not visit me. Children pitied me because my mother never came, but I can remember, miserable as I was, being happy for her—that she was some place where she might find laughter. Only circumstances might have freed her—my father's death, absolute poverty—probably not even these.

The avoidance of pain, of suffering: this has been seen especially to mark American life, and it particularly marks those women who, at the height of the 1965-75 woman's movement, fought its advance. They feared above all the loss of dependence and the discovery of a realm of choice where suffering is possible, even likely.

Until the woman's movement began to change matters in the 1960s, it is fair to say that many American women suffered what Simone Weil called "affliction." Weil identified affliction as having physical, psychological, and social dimensions, an essential condition being that pain must strike in all of these.[21]

From Freud's earliest patients, it is clear that the women's pain has not only a psychological but a physical aspect. Whether marked by headaches, paralysis, whatever—physical effects are clear in women in depression.

The social dimensions of affliction, of course, are the most pervasive: suggesting to women that any revolution against their lot is unnatural, to be punished by expulsion, isolation, displacement, hunger. It is well to be clear about this. Cole Porter, for example, suffered from pain, the result of a riding accident. But this is not affliction, for both psychologically and socially, he prevailed. Virginia Woolf suffered from recurrent bouts of madness, but this is not affliction, because both socially and physically she functioned well, if intermittently. Richard Wright suffered from social pain, but was able, physically and psychologically, to endure it and, by turning it into art, to prevail over it and, in part, end it.

To mention Simone Weil is to be reminded of the obloquy to which women are subjected if they deny themselves the arts thought necessary to their true nature, their "womanliness." Weil refused to adorn herself in any way, refused to allow herself the pride in fashionable dress which, appearing natural, can, nonetheless be the mark of women's slavery, as is the harem.

Adrienne Rich has recently enunciated the source of this disguise that Weil, and only a very few others, consistently shunned. We, as women, Rich writes,

> have been expected to lie with our bodies; to bleach, redden, unkink or curl our hair, pluck eyebrows, shave armpits, wear padding in various places or lace ourselves, take little steps, glaze finger and toe nails, wear clothes that emphasize our helplessness.[22]

Lying, with one's body and one's words is, among the oppressed, a dreadful necessity. Outsiders must often lie to survive. Only women, I think, have also consistently lied to themselves.

3

Women Writers and Female Characters: The Failure of Imagination

Women writers, like successful women in male-dominated professions, have failed to imagine autonomous women characters. With remarkably few exceptions, women writers do not imagine women characters with even the autonomy they themselves have achieved. There is a distinction that must be made here: Margaret Drabble's wish not to be identified with, or confined within, the category of "woman's writer" (to make it as a writer, you must be a man's writer—what could be clearer than that?) is connected with women's inability to imagine women characters, but is not identical with it. Drabble here speaks not as an artist, but like the winners of the Rhodes Scholarships, like one of those who, having achieved a post rare for a woman, denies it is because she is female.

The failure of women writers to imagine female selves as characters is a more profound failure, though it has been recognized as a phenomenon only in the twentieth century. Thus Simone de Beauvoir explains that her novel *The Mandarins* was to contain "all of myself." Yet even in this novel she cannot, she knows, create a positive heroine. "Anna," she writes, "hasn't the autonomy that has been bestowed upon me by a profession which means so much to me." Anna "lives the relative life of a secondary being; Henri resembles me more than Anna does."[1]

Beauvoir had discovered what I also have observed: one *can* act, sometimes shocking oneself at one's courage, or audacity. One lives with the terror, the knowledge of mixed motives and fundamental conflicts, the guilt—but one acts. Yet women writers (and women politicians, academics, psychoanalysts) have been unable to imagine for other women, fictional or real, the self they have in fact achieved. Jane Austen cannot allow her heroines her own unmarried, highly accomplished destiny. Women writers, in short, have articulated their pain. But they cannot, or for the most part have not, imagined characters moving, as the authors themselves have moved, beyond that pain.

Woman's most persistent problem has been to discover for herself an identity not limited by custom or defined by attachment to some man. Remarkably, her search for identity has been even less successful within the world of fiction than outside it, leaving us until very recently with a situation largely unchanged for more than two millenia: men writers have created women characters with autonomy, with a self that is not ancillary, not described by a relationship—wife, mother, daughter, mistress, chief assistant. Women writers, however, when they wished to create an individual filling more than a symbiotic role, projected their ideal of autonomy onto a male character, leaving the heroines to find their role in subservience, or change of name, or both.

The reasons for this are complex, and I do not suppose myself to have named them all: the naming, however, I will postpone for a moment to allow myself to follow the literary process by which women writers reject or abandon the autonomous woman character.

Casting about her for a fictional character in whom to embody what has come to be called "the search for identity," the woman writer is as lost in her creative imagination as she is in life for a knowledge of the process by which a woman could achieve identity, or of what the result might be if she did. Her creative imagination will fail her even when life, in her own case, does not. She therefore projects upon a male character the identity and experience for which she searches, leaving to male authors the creation of female characters who might well be called "heroes."

Male writers, meanwhile, create women characters who achieve a sense of their own selfhood, their own free sense of choosing. Life to these fictional young women presents itself as, in James's words, "dazingly livable." They expend energy in the search for a self, these woman creations of male novelists: Thackeray's Becky Sharp, James's Kate Croy, Lawrence's Ursula Brangwin, Gissing's heroines, Meredith's heroines, Hardy's heroines, Forster's heroines, and on from there. It was not

a bold female poet, but Walt Whitman who wrote of
women:

They are tanned in the face by shining suns and
  blowing winds
Their flesh has the old divine suppleness and strength
They know how to swim, row, ride, wrestle, shoot,
  run, strike, retreat, advance, resist, defend themselves.
They are ultimate in their own right—they are calm,
  clear, well-possessed of themselves.

Not all male writers, it need hardly be said, create
"women heroes." The American male writer, with few
exceptions, has not done so: as in American men generally, the fear of the loss of masculinity is so extreme that
any recognition of a feminine self is unbearably threatening. Among major American writers, before Henry
James, only one male, Hawthorne, ever achieved the creation of an autonomous female character, and he was so
terrified by what he had done that he spent the rest of his
life in fear. European male writers do not all, of course,
create great women characters, any more than all women
writers are concerned with identity or the challenging of
the conventional female role. Nonetheless, it is extraordinary how many male writers have created autonomous
women characters and how few women writers, awake to
the question, have found it possible to resist the creation
of men instead.

An extremely successful and popular woman novelist
whose career perfectly demonstrates the woman writer's
deep need to affirm the patriarchal structure is Mary
Renault. Like other women writers, but more openly,
and to a wider audience, she reveals an author fascinated
with male wholeness, unable to conceive of power as

passing from males in fiction, as it has not passed in life. Renault's early novels, written before her discovery of the all-male Greek world, display awareness of the problem of female autonomy. Yet the struggle is apparently too fundamental for a woman writer, requiring too much of the imagination. Only male writers, it would seem, having undergone one identity crisis, can, in the creation of female characters, risk another.

Renault is commonly mentioned as a writer with a strong interest in homosexuality; certainly her concern with this subject has been present from the beginning and honestly handled in advance of the new permissiveness. But the history of her novels is, more profoundly, the history of a woman writer's struggle to present ideal loves and destinies without the terrible burden of female dependence.

Her six earliest novels had contemporary English settings. The first, *Promise of Love*, is, like many that follow, set in a hospital: Renault, after Oxford, trained to be a nurse. Look-alike brother and sister, with ambiguous names in the manner of Rose Macaulay, are loved by the same man. In the end the brother dies, the sister marries the man and conventionally longs for a baby and her husband's professional success. Renault's second novel, *Kind Are Her Answers*, embarrassingly bad, is also dull because trite; the women are tiresome stereotypes. The third novel, *The Middle Mist*, frankly and courageously presents female homosexuality; yet any chance for female autonomy in these characters is muted. The central male character is hopelessly idealized, and the women are not, as he is, devoted to their professions; they are merely competent, seeing their jobs as compromises. *Return to Night* is, at first, more promising. The central character is a woman doctor, ambitious and willing to face the demands of her profession, higher for a woman. She, however, falls in love with a much younger man and discovers a need to sacrifice herself to him: " 'You're not suggesting I should give up my work? It means as much to me as acting does to you.' As she spoke she realized, with a muffled astonishment, that this statement had become wholly untrue." Her final capitulation to *his* destiny and her love for him are absolute, even though she knows he will eventually tire of her:

> Hilary, for her part, was recalling the ambitions and the indignations which had seemed important to her a year or two ago. It was as if somebody had repeated to her a very old joke, of which she had only just seen the point. How anxious she had been to prove that she could get an appointment over David's head! To do this, it had seemed, would prove something or other about women and men. It was excruciatingly funny to think she might have got it—or the presidency of the College of Surgeons, for that matter—only to find herself exactly where she now was. The hard core for a feminist to bite on had, after all, been something as simple as this. . . . Now for the first time it was borne in on her, like a piece of news, that being a woman was a fact about which absolutely nothing could be done. She had spent so long in battle with non-essentials; the essential had stolen up on her unaware.

Is it any wonder that, with such a view of woman's inevitable destiny as subservient passion, Renault should have looked for action to the world of men alone? Especially since she tended to see men as victimized by the love of women.

North Face, the fifth novel, is again conventional, with stereotyped women (to which the "old maid" figure has been added) and intense friendships between men. These friendships turn to sexual love in *The Charioteer,* her final English novel. Taking its title from *The Phaedrus,* this novel relegates annoying women characters to minor roles and explores problems of relationships with a cast of males. The hero thinks of women as Nazis and dreams of Athens. Deciding not to live with his lover, he thinks: "He wants to be brave for me too; and no one can do that." Every woman should aspire to that sentence, but Renault could not imagine one doing so.

The Last of the Wine, set in ancient Greece, freed her imagination from the necessity of sex stereotypes, not because women had different roles in ancient Greece, but because they could be conceived as having no roles at all. The lovers in this book refer to women simply as property, as in the Ten Commandments. Renault found herself free to play out ideals of love and destiny with no concessions to the troublesome female struggle for identity. Oddly, boys took the place of the girls of pre-World War I England, with tutors instead of governesses to protect them from lascivious males. Xantippe is twice confirmed in her shrewishness, though neither Plato nor Xenophon gives any basis for this long tradition. Like the brilliant women who worked with Freud, like women Freudian analysts since, like most successful women in past years, Renault became an apologist for female subservience. The lovers speak to one another:

Tell me this, Lysis; where do you think the soul goes when we die?

Who has come back to tell us? Perhaps, as Pythagoras taught, into the womb again. Into a philosopher if we deserved it, or a woman if we were weak; or a beast or bird if we failed altogether to be men.

The King Must Die reaches back to the legend of Theseus, who sets out deliberately to overthrow women rul-

ers, the worship of female gods, and the male role of
consort to the Queen. Yet when Theseus sails for Crete
with his team of boy and girl bull dancers, he conceives
of the girls as an integral, essential part of the team's
success: they achieve equality and even esteem as ath-
letes. Renault seems to move, given the possibility within
her material of such an interpretation, toward the creation of women of achievement.

The Bull from the Sea, the sequel, provides Renault's
only attempt at a major autonomous woman character.
The myth of the Amazons gave her Hippolyte. Yet the
equality Hippolyte finds as Theseus's consort is a gift
from him; their "marriage" is one of equals, which he
can allow since his male dominance has been established. Perhaps this would seem a prophetic scheme,
looking forward, with hope, toward a possible future
when men might no longer have to prove themselves and
women might develop high skills. Alas, Hippolyte ends
as "a woman to the last," sacrificing herself in the place
of her husband, in an insistence upon self-immolation
that he recognizes as in conflict with his destiny. Much
might have been hoped for from Renault's one wholly
heterosexual hero. Yet here again, the creation of a
woman hero is deflected; the unusual destiny of an individual refusing the stereotyped role is given to Hip-
polytus, who is safely male. Interestingly, Antigone is
twice deprecated in this novel, as Xantippe had earlier
been.

The Mask of Apollo, recreating the acting profession in
the third century B.C., demonstrates prophetically for
literature that the creation of women roles, that high art,
is the proper work of men. Again there is what would
have been, between a man and woman, an idealized
"marriage" between actors. The only female is one of

two historical women students in Plato's academy. Axio-
thea confides to the hero her grief at not being able to
go to war with the male students:

> I must have done wrong in my last life on earth, and this is
> the punishment I chose when my eyes were opened. So I
> ought to bear it patiently, and hope for better next time. But,
> oh, it is hard.

Renault finds it easy to agree with Plato in his epigraph
to Dion, that all women are "spun into the dark web on
the day of their birth."

The novels about Alexander, *Fire from Heaven* and *The
Persian Boy*, return again to an all-male world of armies,
where women are raped and murdered. The role of "female" lover is played by the Persian eunuch who, though
idealized in the degree of servitude he offers Alexander,
can assert his manliness by accompanying the army on
the campaigns.

It is, obviously, ungrateful to criticize Renault in the
face of her considerable accomplishment: her novels are
readable and intelligent, and they create with great imagination a past world. Should we ask that she create a
possible future world also? Yet we cannot help but notice
that many women novelists, Renault among them, have
themselves achieved an autonomy they deny their heroines.

Equally indicative of the female urge toward the destruction and denial of female destiny is the woman novelist who manages to achieve an autonomous woman
character in perhaps one or two novels, and then relin-
quishes the central role to men. Willa Cather is such an
author. Like many modern women writers, she used a
male protagonist in her first novel, but with her second

novel, *O Pioneers!*, she found a woman hero. "In his daughter," Cather writes,

> John Bergson recognized the strength of will, and the simple direct way of thinking things out, that had characterized his father in his better days. He would much rather, of course, have seen this likeness in one of his sons, but it was not a question of choice. As he lay there day after day he had to accept the situation as it was, and to be thankful that there was one among his children to whom he could entrust the future of his family and the possibilities of his hard-won land.

Her next novel, *The Song of the Lark*, is of a woman artist, a singer, Thea Kronberg, who fulfills the destiny of achievement. Cather recognizes the centrality of passion to such an achievement and the necessity, harder for a woman, to stop giving in relationships merely for the sake of giving and to preserve the valuable self. Maurice Beebe, in his study of the artist in literature, *Ivory Towers and Sacred Founts*, finds few fictional artists who sacrifice life entirely to their art.[2] Thea Kronberg is the only example he offers. When Thea is reproached for having so little private life, she replies:

> I don't have any. Your work becomes your personal life. You are not much good until it does. It's like being woven into a big web. You can't pull away, because all your little tendrils are woven into the picture. It takes you up, and uses you, and spins you out; and that is your life. Not much else can happen to you.

But in *The Song of the Lark* Cather's struggle is becoming evident: the prose slackens. She was later to cut the book, to write an apologetic preface, to worry about its form.

Thea Kronberg, therefore, is Cather's last major woman character with a "self."

My Antonia, her next novel, shows us a strong and vital woman. But the first person narration has been given to a man, and the last sight we have of Antonia is triumphant—as the mother of sons. (The final section is called, significantly, "Cuzaks' Boys.") After *My Antonia* the struggle is over, the imagination has failed in its creation of women, and has shifted to male heroes. *One of Ours,* a war novel, exalts war as an experience for the hero, who is, needless to say, male. *A Lost Lady* shows women as defaced property, like the land, put to shameful uses when proper male dominance falters. *The Professor's House* has a male protagonist as do, of course, the two patriarchal Catholic novels, *Death Comes for the Archbishop* and *Shadows on the Rock.* Both of these works exalt the patriarchal order, and although there is a father-daughter relationship in *Shadows on the Rock,* the daughter is a surrogate wife. She fulfills her destiny, like Antonia, by providing her apothecary father with four grandsons—no time to waste on daughters here.

It is extraordinarily puzzling that the identity crisis through which an accomplished woman author passes with evident success should so strongly resist imaginative recreation. As a recent critic has observed about an earlier, greater woman novelist:

What is fatally hampering to George Eliot's heroines is not society, not even provincial society, but their own lack of creativity, which includes creative intellectual powers. Obstacles of all kinds are put in their way, it is true, and George Eliot makes us feel so sorry for them that we overlook the fact that in real life, given the motivation and the talent, women could and did overcome them. George Eliot herself tri-

umphed over greater handicaps than any of her women characters are faced with.[3]

Yet the female imagination does not falter in the creation of male characters. Edith Wharton, for example,
never in her fiction depicts women artists whose lives
might reflect her own struggle. Cynthia Wolff, in her
study of Edith Wharton, points out that the artists in
Wharton's work "were usually men, and women appear
as agreeable subjects for them or as more or less sufficient attendants to the muse. What profound ambivalence and fierce reticence this lifelong preoccupation
suggests!" When, later in her career, Wharton began to
write novels focusing on the two elements postulated by
Freud as essential to happiness, love, and work, she "always employed a male protagonist. Never a woman."
Wolff explains that Wharton can delineate the nature of
an ambitious woman by suggesting "what she would
have done *if she had been a man.*" Given that her heroine
was a woman, however, her ambitions "must be rendered by a series of domestic virtues." Since attractive
and "natural" women cannot possess the "masculine"
trait of assertiveness, it follows that any character pos-
sessing it must be a man.[4]

Many women novelists display a preference not only
for the male hero but also for the masculine voice. Diana
Trilling detected such a tendency in 1965:

> In *The Benefactor,* the recent first novel of a young woman
> writer of notable gift, Susan Sontag, there is nothing in ei-
> ther its matter or manner to suggest the sex of its author.
> Not only is the central character a man but a man who is
> the very personification of depersonalization. . . . For the
> most part, the present-day serious female writer echoes
> the male voice.[5]

Sontag's next novel also has a male protagonist, and in this novel, as in the first, the female character is mutilated. Although Sontag has moved, in her published writings, into a more feminist position—and, indeed, her advice to women on this subject is absolutely central[6]—she has not managed to create a female protagonist.

A preference for the masculine voice is seen even more clearly in the novels of Iris Murdoch. By 1976, she had published eighteen of them. Of these, thirteen are written in the third person. Five, including the first, *Under the Net,* are written in the first person, always male. Although there are occasional women characters who do more than move, with varying degrees of dependency from one love affair or marriage to the next, the action in the novels is heavily vested in the male characters. It might also be noted, parenthetically, that Murdoch's male homosexuals are treated with considerably more range and humor than are her female homosexuals.

Similarly, E. Nesbit (she always used the initial) was flattered to be thought a man, an impression she tried to confirm by writing all first-person stories in the masculine character.[7]

Penelope Mortimer, a fine and underesteemed novelist, might be cited as a current exception: a woman novelist, all of whose protagonists are women—indeed, women with many children. But in a larger sense she is no exception, for all her protagonists suffer a notable lack of selfhood. Only one has the single element that has preserved Mortimer's own life: her work. That single working heroine, in *My Friend Says It's Bullet Proof,* has been mutilated, before the book begins, by a mastectomy.[8]

Pauline Kael recently wondered, in print, why a

woman as strong as Lillian Hellman should have deferred constantly to the masculine point of view:

In "Turtle" [one of Hellman's autobiographical accounts
from *Pentimento*] there are only two important characters—
Hellman and Hammett, with whom she lived off and on for
almost thirty years—and it's evident that for him strong and
clear and definite meant masculine, while doubts and un-
resolved feelings were weak nonsense: feminine. Lillian
Hellman tried to write (and to live) in a way that Hammett
would approve of; he rejected much of what she actually
felt, and she accepted his standards. (The question of why a
woman of such strength and, in many ways, of such ruthless
honesty should have deferred to the judgment of a man of
lesser gifts than her own—that's the sexual mystery that
would make a drama.)[9]

The female writer, even when writing of animals,
seems to conceive of the love of adventure as male. Does
not Beatrix Potter clearly prefer Peter and Benjamin to
Flopsy, Mopsy, and Cottontail, those good bunnies, who
stay home and behave, being female?

Charlotte Brontë, it is true, stands as a major exception to the pattern of failed imagination: at the culmina-
tion of her career she created Lucy Snow in *Villette,* an
autonomous woman standing alone. But, as Helene
Moglen has shown, the heroines in Brontë's earliest
fiction defined themselves, as women had always been
driven to do, by their dependency on men. Brontë's
women in the early stories, Moglen writes,

are defined by their capacity for love; but they never love or
esteem themselves. They depend upon their dependency.
For them the greatest horror is not the physical loss of their
lovers—but the psychological loss: to have autonomy thrust

upon them—to be forced back into the void of the self. Alone, they barely exist.[10]

The phrase "the void of the self," which so sharply defines most women deprived of male support, stands in opposition to what John Mack has called, in writing of T.E. Lawrence, "the exquisite realization of the self."[11] One may, of course, choose a certain dependency after the realization of the self, but one must first conceive that such a realization is indeed "exquisite."

Among those women writers who struggle through, as Brontë did, to a sense of her own capabilities and even the imagination of a fictional heroine who possesses them, there is more often than not, as in women generally, a concomitant despising of women. The resources of scorn toward other females that the achieving woman has been able to call upon seem, outside of the historical periods of feminism, to be nearly bottomless. Diane Johnson observes that Charlotte Brontë, in her later years of fame, discovered

> even women she respected, like Mrs. Gaskell and Harriet Martineau, [to be] involved in a strange collaboration to misrepresent female nature. . . . Indeed, in all her writing, Charlotte Brontë, who was no more charitable than Jane Austen in her treatment of fools of either sex, reserved particular scorn for women. She understood how society made them what they were ("envious, backbiting, wretched"), but she seemed to despise them, perhaps because she more than most people knew them to be capable of manliness.[12]

Gertrude Stein, too, knew herself to be capable of "manliness." Catharine Stimpson has elucidated Stein's movement from "the younger Stein who celebrated the new woman who would be wife, mother, and economic boon," to the older writer separating herself from this new woman "in order to assail and herself enter a male world too strong for most women."[13]

Whatever the reasons or rationalizations for this movement, it has marked the careers of countless achieving women. Even a woman whose own work has contributed to a feminist revolution can be tempted by subtle demands for her skill and cooperation to desert women's cause at the very height of the movement, and enter "a male world too strong for most women." Almost inevitably, the accomplished woman will be tempted to complete her own development by attention to what the society conceives as the central question, rather than by persisting in work that is in any way related to her position as a woman. One thinks of Margaret Fuller, striving continually to find a destiny for women that would free them from domesticity and allow them a life of high accomplishment, fulfilling herself ultimately in the Italian revolutionary struggle rather than in an enterprise devoted to women.

Well, why not? Isn't it natural and even desirable that a successful woman should move from involvement with the female condition to involvement with the human condition? To agree, however, is to overlook the unhappy fact that in all aspects of our culture, the feminine element has been so long ignored that movement toward apparently "human" concerns is in fact movement back into a cultural tradition still dominated by male-centered values. The question must certainly arise: is there a woman's angle to everything? The answer at this stage is, yes, there is.

Men in our male-centered culture consistently ignore the perspective of female experience. They study classical psychoanalysis, or the nuclear family, for example, only to idealize the conventional role of the mother, not to examine it. Women who have entered the male-dominated world of work or the professions unaware of their womanhood, unidentified with women, convinced that all knowledge is sexually neutral, not only fail in their duty to other women but perhaps also in their obligation to their own work. Let me speculate on the case of Hannah Arendt.

I met her only once, when we were both members of a large special seminar at Columbia. I cannot now recall its subject—indeed that was far from clear even at the time—but Hannah Arendt spoke and she was, as ever, profound and stimulating. She mentioned to me that this was one of the few occasions in her life when she had not been the only woman in such a gathering. I did not respond, having heard from other women who had approached her on the subject that she scorned feminism.

In her volume *Work,* Arendt's distinction between work and labor perfectly described the complete absence of humanity in the household labor to which so many women are confined. Yet in her posthumous book entitled *Thinking,* it seems never to have occurred to her that thinking and its absence may be fundamentally connected with imposed sex roles in our society. I would argue that the quality of many women's thinking—its confined scope and unambitious character, its lack of clarity and penetration—is shaped by the passivity and submissiveness to which they have been conventionally trained. An unwillingness to "think" in Arendt's sense of that term has been precisely inculcated by "female" upbringing. This same unwillingness helps to account for the role of women as conservatives in this world, as defenders of the conventional even when mistreatment of women is the result. For example, public opinion polls show that a higher proportion of women than men oppose passage of the Equal Rights Amendment. Women's support has probably been essential to the success of conservative movements in the United States and elsewhere. That support has been won so readily not just because conservatives play upon women's fears, but also because women have, in effect, been trained not to *think*, even about their own situation. Thus, fundamental political events may well be shaped by the quality of women's thought. Yet this notion would not occur to Hannah Arendt because she had adopted the male perspective as though it were naturally and exclusively appropriate to every investigation.

Implicit in Arendt's work, and in much of social thought as well, is the notion that the male perspective equals the human and therefore also encompasses the assumedly narrower female view. For women novelists, as we have seen, the corollary of this appears to be the assumption that only a male character can stand for the full range of human experience, moving through action and quest to achievement or failure.

Just as society assumes the male view to be all encompassing and the female restricted, so it also tolerates a wide range of behavior in men while insisting on a much narrower scope for women. I do not here refer to jobs and occupations—whether women ought to be bus drivers, soldiers, or airline pilots, though of course they should—but to social manners, the way we behave in whatever occupations we perform. The range of permissible male behavior includes the charming and, indeed, anything not absolutely characterized as "feminine." Female behavior, on the other hand, when conventionally "unfeminine" is condemned as offensive. A prominent editor in New York said to me casually at lunch, for example, that male homosexuals are charming and gay and delightful, while women homosexuals are hairy and ponderous and thumpy. Here is a choice example of the "no-win" situation women are forced into by conventional opinion. For if homosexual men—by which the editor seemed to mean men who proclaim their homosexuality in their gestures, speech, etc.—are charming, gay, and delightful, why are not forthright, hard-boiled women also refreshing and delightful? The answer is, of course, that, in the conventional view, all male action is capable of charm, while only proper female action is even acceptable.

Worse yet, in the conventional view, propriety must constrain women not only in their personal behavior but also in the world of politics. As clergymen in the nineteenth century said to women: "Stay within your proper confines, and you will be worshipped; . . . step outside, and you will cease to exist."[14] That this "Victorian" view has persisted down to the present moment is nicely illustrated by Aileen Kelly in an article on Eleanor Marx. Kelly tells us that the qualities of Eleanor Marx's personality combined in a kind of harmony rare in public-minded women of the Victorian period. Almost all the women in public life—a minute number—were "pioneers in the movement for female emancipation [who] tended to assume a defensive armor of self-conscious stridency or studied eccentricity." Eleanor Marx, on the other hand, had a deep sensitivity to suffering, and felt that the misery of the poor required action from her which "she believed should take priority over the exclusive causes, such as that of women's emancipation." Kelly does not claim that Marx, in fact, accomplished much for the poor. Nonetheless, she clearly condones,

indeed applauds, the choice of priorities. The emphasis
is not accidental; at the close of the article, when Kelly
praises Eleanor Marx for shouting herself hoarse calling
on the men to stand and fight on Bloody Sunday, she
remarks that this same "kind of militancy on the part of
the leaders of the women's movement would subsequently be very largely a personal statement or a *strident*
gesture of group self-assertion." The word strident, borrowed from the male arsenal, is used against those in the
cause of women. Those in the cause of men are seen as
"devoid of self-consciousness—her energies were con-
centrated outside herself, on a cause which was not her
own."[15] Apparently the double standard continues to
apply in politics, even after it has been abandoned in the
bedroom.

In a world where such judgments continue to be made,
it is scarcely surprising that women writers have not attempted the struggle to present their own accomplishment as women fictively. Yet it must be granted that, at
least among women writers of today's feminist generation, there are signs of change: increasingly women writers are able to create women characters who can articulate their pain, and to imagine women characters who
have acquired characteristics hitherto labeled masculine.
Gail Godwin articulates woman's condition convincingly
in her second novel, *The Glass People,* for example, where
the heroine says: "It's as though I want some final force
to enter me and take over my body, set me on some
genuine destiny that can't be changed, that I can't turn
back from." Later, the same woman asks plaintively:
"Does a person always have to go out and seek destiny?
Perhaps my destiny will come and seek me." Godwin's
later novels are extraordinary in their development of
female heroes who are not only aware of the need for an

independent destiny, but struggling toward it. Lois
Gould's *A Sea Change* is also an example of a courageous
and fascinating attempt to write out the central problem
of the female consciousness in revolt at being victimized.
(Those critics I am familiar with have not, however, been
very perspicacious in their reviews of either of these
novelists' work.)

Women poets, more than women novelists, have
found the lyrical voice for their own sense of themselves,
for their anger, their particular isolation. It seems likely,
moreover, that poetry is capable of expressing quintes-
sentially a certain balancing of tension, the holding in the
mind for a moment in perfect balance two otherwise
incompatible ideas, which allows greater bravery than
does the novel, because the bravery is momentary, however marvelous.

Adrienne Rich has realized what poetry can express,
but what becomes somehow too attenuated and trying in
fiction: the particular strength of women. She sees no
reason why, because patriarchy calls something by a
pejorative name, you must think of it as a negative value.
Weak-ego boundaries in women are, she points out, a
negative way of describing women's "tremendous powers of intuitive identification similar to Keats's negative
capability." Such loss of ego, Rich suggests, might, for
a poet, be a source of power.[16] (Do we not observe that
power in Emily Dickinson?) Denise Levertov has bravely
captured a sense of female striving for autonomy in a
lyric expression:

> In childhood dream-play I was always
>   the knight or squire, not
>   the lady:

quester, petitioner, win or lose, not
she who was sought.
The initial of quest or question
branded itself long since on the flank
of my Pegasus.
Yet he flies always
home to the present.

But until the years of the recent feminist movement,
to tell the story, to continue the quest, to follow through
the plot of accomplishment in an extended work of
fiction has been all but impossible for women writers.
Women may, let us suppose, have read Thoreau: "I have
learned this at least in my experiment: that if one advances confidently in the direction of his dreams, and
endeavors to live the life which he has imagined, he will
meet with a success unexpected in common hours." But
their failure was a prior one: the inability even to imagine
a life in which a woman, without clothing herself in the
character of a man, yet goes forth, full of hope and purpose, into a world that men have always dominated. Margaret Fuller prophesied: "The Woman in me kneels and
weeps in tender rapture; the Man in me rushes forth, but
only to be baffled. Yet the time will come when, from the
union of this tragic king and queen, shall be born a
radiant sovereign self."[17] Her prophecy is not yet
fulfilled either in life or in fiction.

4

Search for a Model: Female Childhood

In academic circles, nothing has so clearly marked the current woman's movement as the search for female role models through the recovery of female history. Despite the dismissive snorts and defensive sneers of male scholars not eager to be told that their past labors had excluded consideration of half the human race, women historians—and some male scholars as well—began the enormous task of uncovering the hidden history of women. At the same time, women literary scholars set out to bring before the consciousness of their critical and scholarly colleagues the works of formerly unknown women, new interpretations of the life and work of women writers, and a sense of the relationship between the major literary women of the past.[1] In the fields of religion and anthropology, a search went on for new interpretations of women's role in church and culture.

If scholars in the disciplines of psychology and sociology examined the future—ways in which women might enact a different, less constrained destiny—those in disciplines whose subject was the past wrestled with the angel of reinterpretation, refusing to desist until they had wrenched from that angel the blessing from the female past upon the female future.

Women engaged in these studies have found them fascinating and without doubt a source of strength, inspiration, and enlightenment. It is, furthermore, a matter of the greatest importance, understood by feminists everywhere, that women should learn to examine and to speak from their own experience, no longer content to feel, judge, and act exclusively according to the modes and standards deemed appropriate in a patriarchal cultural tradition. At the level of social and psychological theory, as I shall argue presently, we need the insights of the Karen Horneys of this world to correct the errors of a learned establishment misled by its own exclusively masculine perspective. Equally important, the individual woman must learn to recognize and to value her own experience and to articulate her true condition.

Certainly these endeavors must and will continue. Yet I am convinced that something more is needed, as well. If women are now to enter the male-dominated world as full participants and in large numbers, they cannot do so by building exclusively on contemporary female experience galvanized by the example of those female role models available in the present or recaptured, however joyfully, from the past.

They must have a stronger psychological base, a wider foothold, than can be provided by female experience alone. The reinvention of womanhood, I think, requires chiefly an effort to widen its boundaries and enlarge its scope. If women can take as their own the creative possibilities, the human aspirations once the property of men only, can they not also adopt male role models in their struggle for achievement? I believe that women must learn to appropriate for their own use the examples of human autonomy and self-fulfillment displayed to us by the male world.

Need I add that the imitation of men should not be slavish—more in the spirit of Aristotle's mimesis than of the modern, largely pejorative sense of the word? True imitation of an action, Aristotle has taught us, consists in discovering its spirit, its essential energy, and reforming that into another, mimetic action.

That, as they say, is a tall order. It will require the remaining pages of this book to explain its meaning, support it with evidence, draw out its implications. Let me here explain that meaning and sketch those implications in the most summary fashion. Adopting male models of achievement has implications both for the individual woman and for the woman's movement. For individual women, it means not accepting the limitations of "proper behavior" or of "female destiny" but insisting that women can seek any human goal; it means not depending only on female role models as they now exist but also adopting male role models in the search for selfhood.

Forster understood as long ago as 1905 how a young woman might long for an unconfined destiny, as she sees it in the male world, without believing she herself must become masculine to enjoy it. "Why are most big things unladylike?" Lucy wonders in *A Room with a View.*

In her heart there were always springing up strange desires. She too is enamoured of heavy winds, and vast panoramas, and green expanses of the sea. She has marked the kingdom of this world, how full it is of wealth, and beauty, and war. . . . Men, declaring that she inspires them to it, move joyfully over the surface, having the most delightful meetings with other men, happy, not because they are masculine, but because they are alive.

For the individual woman, adopting male models also means rejecting the Freudian interpretation of the special nature of women's personality development, in favor of the view that the Oedipal process marks out a path by which women, as well as men, can achieve maturity and independence.

Since Freud, woman has been supposed to envy male genitals, profoundly desiring either to possess or to destroy them. This view has done women more damage as supposition than it would have as truth: it is easier to fight dragons than chimeras. What woman does envy and should envy is male destiny—to possess it, and to destroy that part of it inimical to herself.

For women in their social relationships and for the woman's movement, adopting male models of achievement has several implications. Socially, it means not accepting a unique responsibility in childcare, but insisting that new institutions, including new family arrangements, be developed to allow full male participation in child rearing. How the family might be restructured and what effect that might have on the personality development of the young are questions reserved for a separate chapter.

Politically, following the male example of accomplishment means not allowing the purposes of the woman's movement to be set aside in favor of any other objectives, but insisting, as male-dominated movements have done, on the paramount importance of the group's own political aims. The history of the woman's movement is the history of ends repeatedly put aside for other purposes deemed temporarily more important: in the United States before 1860, the abolition of slavery; in England in the late nineteenth century, the rights of labor; in the present, perhaps, the primacy of infant nurture or the rights of ethnic minorities. Women have behaved not as an oppressed class struggling to overcome their oppression, but as a caste, identifying with their oppressors, internalizing the oppressors' views of them. Since men do not take women's rights seriously, most women also refuse to do so. Until women adopt a model for action that sustains the primacy of their own claims, they will not achieve full equality.

I recognize that these prescriptions contain apparent contradictions and paradoxes. For example, if women adopt the male pattern of achievement, must they take on its meaner aspects as well? I would answer that the meaner aspects of competitive male behavior are despicable in men and would be equally so in women. But to insist that women shun competitive behavior solely for that reason is to condemn women to continued failure, while doing nothing to redeem the sins of the male.

Or, if women embrace the male role model for achievement, doesn't that imply that they will cease to think of themselves as women and no longer support either the woman's movement or other individual women following after them in job or profession? My answer is that women must appropriate aspects of male behavior to themselves *as women,* enlarging the scope of womanhood in the process, so that what they choose to do is now defined as womanly rather than manly. Step-by-step with this redefinition of boundaries, women's imagination of possible female destinies will expand; women writers will at last be able to imagine women as heroes. Moreover, when successful women in every job and profession think of themselves as women rather than as honorary males, their sympathy with other women will expand, too.

Finally, if women adopt the male model of achievement, does that mean suspending the reexamination of history and myth that is now carried forward eagerly by women scholars, who hope to recover or reveal the lost or hidden history of women? The answer, as I shall try to show in the next chapter, is that the reinterpretation of history and myth is one of the most powerful means women have of demonstrating their historic fitness to play all the roles in the human drama.

Is not the experience of gender, particularly in the light of Freud's discovery of the operations of the unconscious, so "set," biologically and psychologically so determined, that to speak of male models for women is to suggest either an absurdity or else the sort of perversion that haunts, one supposes, the dreams of Anita Bryant?

It is, of course, unclear at what point Freudian studies will break through the prison of gender and recognize that the unconscious can be retained without what has always been considered the centerpiece of Freudian determinism, the sex of the child. My own experience of psychoanalysis, consisting entirely in acquaintanceship and conversation, suggests that the present generation of psychoanalysts are unlikely to abandon the classic Freudian model with anything that might be considered haste, or even with what the Supreme Court once called "all deliberate speed."

The men of my own generation and earlier who chose to be analysts tended to be a certain type. Profoundly fearful of women, they were drawn irresistibly to a philosophy that reinforced their earliest fears and most passionate hopes. Supporting the conventions of sexuality and sex roles to a degree not later exceeded by Phyllis Schlafly and the Mormon Church, they were typically patriarchal in welcoming into their ranks "token" women who echoed their most profoundly masculinist theories, and whom they rewarded with honorary membership in the male community. Indeed, the history of the psychoanalytic movement in America is a model of how patriarchal institutions work. It provides the ultimate answer to "token" women in whatever field, who continue to insist, from the example of their own success, that "there's really no problem."

The only valid test is provided by women such as Horney, who do not echo the male point of view, but speak as women from their own experience. When Horney refused tokenism and offered dialogue instead, the patriarchs turned her out of the club. Women psychoanalysts such as Helene Deutsch or Phyllis Greenacre, to take but two examples of those who remained within the establishment, propounded doctrinaire Freudian theories of womanhood that in no way reflected their own extraordinary careers as women but were based instead, on the observation of "others"; they themselves, presumably, were not "women" within the statutory meaning of that term.

In 1974 there occurred what was for me the first rea-
soned psychoanalytic argument against Freud's account
of female development: in the *Journal of the American Psychoanalytic Association,* Roy Schafer expounded upon
"Problems in Freud's Psychology of Women." He explained, in psychoanalytic terms *and* in a psychoanalytic
journal, what I had always known in my gut, that
"Freud's estimates of women's morality and objectivity
are logically conventional patriarchal values and judgments that have been misconstrued as being disinter-
ested, culture-free scientific observations."[2]

The problem for me had been that, while Freud's discussions of women had seemed incredibly biased, both
in their phallocentricity and in their slighting of the
mother's role in the development of the child, I had
inevitably found it impossible to discuss with any psychoanalyst the suggestion that Freud could have been
wrong about women, even though I was not challenging
the profundity and accuracy of his essential discoveries.
The expulsion of Horney still represents their response
to a bid for the reexamination of women's psychic development. Schafer's article seemed little less than the gift
of hope.

And then, just after I had read Schafer's article, Juliet
Mitchell's *Psychoanalysis and Feminism*[3] was published.
Mitchell's is a passionate defense of Freud's theories
about women and an attack on those feminists who, outside of the precincts of psychoanalysis, had tried to discuss them. Mitchell's book plunged me into gloom. It
seemed a made-to-order illustration of women's alarm-
ing tendency to return, after a few daring forays, to the
safe harbor of male opinion. I had often noticed how
women who enter analysis and the study of Freud's theories commit themselves, with a passion not unlike that of

nuns to the service of Christ, to unquestioning belief. A desire to lose the troublesome, anxiety-producing self is certainly an element in this process; as women, they need no longer struggle beyond what appears an allotted destiny. The male club rewards allegiance with both professional status and escape from anxiety.

Mitchell had restated Freud's theories, believing them to be accurate in their account of female development in a patriarchal world. Her criticism of feminist objections to Freud and her apparent suggestions for ways out of this prison of gender, if indeed she was ready to seek a way out, were weak, confused, and inadequate. At the same time, her restatement of Freud's theories, like Deutsch's observations of female development, was brilliant.

I was rescued from despair after Mitchell's book by a review of it by Sherry Ortner, who showed the direction in which we might move. "The process of maleness and femaleness, as articulated by Freud," Ortner wrote, "is precisely that—a *process* of development. Male and female babies have, according to Freud, the same physical structure. . . . In Freud's theory, females are not attributed with some a priori maternal instinct, or some a priori tendency to be nurturant; all of these tendencies emerge later, as the outcome of female experience in the Oedipal process."

Ortner accepts the importance of the Oedipal complex, and argues for retaining it as a theory. "It is a powerful and, significantly, an eminently dialectical theory: the person evolves through a process of struggle with and ultimate supercession (including integration) of symbolic figures of love, desire, authority."[4] The process prepares the individual for the development both of personality and of social role. Ortner concludes, however, that the Freudian model must be revised to acknowledge that the girl as well as the boy is capable of partaking of the process of individual integration in the highest degree.

In a later section, I shall try to examine the ways in which the family might be reconceived to enable more symmetrical development between males and females, and rescue each from the deprivations now inherent in our system of infant nurture. In the study of the problems of mothering as it is presently understood, and has been practiced for centuries, I was encouraged, in the years following the Ortner review, first by Dorothy Dinnerstein's *The Mermaid and the Minotaur,*[5] and then by Nancy Chodorow's *The Reproduction of Mothering.* Dinnerstein's book presented the whole problem of exclusive female mothering with energy and imagination; Chodorow, on whose work I have extensively relied, examined the Freudian model of infant development with consistent method, great clarity, and thoroughness.

Meanwhile, the whole meaning of "identity," and the general failure of women to discover it for themselves, could now be fruitfully defined and examined in the light of revisions in psychoanalytic theory that predated Schafer's article. These new interpretations have made little headway in the culture generally; they are crucial, however, to an understanding of women's struggle to achieve selfhood.

Freud's discovery, not alone of the patterns of the unconscious, but of the stages of early development culminating in the Oedipal phase, made apparent the process by which the child, from birth onward, undergoes and survives the tensions between himself, his parents, and the society as a whole. The magnificence of Freud's discovery lay in his recognition of this process. The terrible, and terribly different burdens he cast upon males and females, however, evolved from an inevitably male-centered view of the human condition. He did not, of course, invent it: it lay, from his infancy, all about him. He saw the male child as successfully able to accomplish that passage known as the Oedipal crisis, precisely because—and this was of greatest importance to later interpretations—he believed the male child to be in the correct, or ideal, relation to the mother. Of the opposite sex from his mother, the boy was able to consider himself as her lover and, potentially, as the lover of women. Freud went astray, as we now know, not in his observation of data, but in his interpretation of it. The unfortunate consequences of this have followed, not from Freud's misinterpretations alone (these were certainly understandable in a man of Victorian origins), but from the persistence with which succeeding generations of psychoanalysts have, with the tenacity of Aristotelians, insisted upon the literal accuracy of Freud's *particular* interpretations rather than upon the brilliance with which he revealed previously unimagined processes in human development. Nor has the Freudian establishment yet found itself ready to incorporate the new findings in a meaningful way. Their special "Catch-22"—if you cannot believe the classical Freudian interpretation, it is because you are neurotic—has saved them the bother of confronting new ideas.

Four discoveries have, nonetheless, brought the problem of female identification closer to our understanding. One is the realization that the so-called basic sex is not male as Freud thought, but female; every fetus starts female. Second is the discovery that sexual identity for a child, what has come to be called "core gender identity," is not biological, but assigned: if the child has not been identified as definitely one sex or the other by the age of three, nothing but disaster can follow; it is the assignment, however, that is important, not the biological sex.[6] Third is the realization that the male child, not the female, has the hardest adjustment in maturation: the infant's first desire is to be the mother, to identify with her. For a girl child, this first, overpowering infant identity need never shift; for a boy child that shift will be essential. This leads, in my view, to a fourth complex of insights. The problem for the boy, as analysts now recognize, is that the shift in gender identification is not easily made.[7] The male, therefore, may suffer many forms of sexual dysfunction as a direct result of this switch: extreme homosexuality, impotence, transvestitism, perversion, fetishism, sado-masochism, etc. The female, secure in her sexual identity, suffers few if any of these. Her problems, I believe, arise precisely from the lack of struggle, from the fact that she need never undergo an identity crisis, and indeed, is almost incapable of one.

All societies, from the earliest and most primitive to today's, have ceremoniously taken the boy from the female domain and urged his identity as a male, as a responsible unfeminine individual, upon him. The girl undergoes no such ceremony, but she pays for serenity of passage with a lack of selfhood and of the will to autonomy that only the struggle for identity can confer. The male undergoes a profound identity struggle, but often pays for it with sexual dysfunction.

The girl, thus, has passed, all too easily, from infantile identity with the mother to complete identity with her. If she comes to hate this mother she may, as an adult, suffer frigidity, postpartum depression, or a dislike of women. These conditions need not, however, affect, as a man's sexual dysfunction must affect, her entire personality adjustment. The price of this easier personality adjustment, allowed her because of her identity with her mother, is high: her autonomy. Stoller, expressing the classical Freudian view, tells us that biological bisexuality "produces an unalterable part of human psychology, which leads in men to a fear of not being manly, and in women an urge to be manly."[8] To the classical analyst, this means that a man fears the loss of his penis, while the woman desires one. To the modern, nonclassical Freudian, it can mean that the man struggles, at high cost, through to an identity; while the woman, her struggle called unfeminine, recognizes the need for an identity crisis, but cannot discover a way to achieve it, nor even the form it is likely to take. Society has generally provided her with no female model but the nurturing, ultimately deserted mother.

It would seem clear that the psychological instability of the boy and the failure of self-differentiation of the girl suggest one solution: the father's active role in child care, the mother's role as worker in the outer world among peers. Such an arrangement would, among its many benefits, protect future generations of children from the rigid sex-role stereotyping, which among developed nations is more enforced in the United States than elsewhere.[9] The discussion of restructuring the family and marriage, however, deserves a chapter of its own; I return to it in Chapter 6.

The difficulty women generally have encountered in achieving identity, that is, a sense of themselves as autonomous, self-directed individuals, might well be expected to have prevented them from successfully pursuing careers in an essentially hostile—because male-dominated —society. Yet, obviously, against all odds, some women *have* achieved eminence, been accounted successes by whatever worldly standards one chooses to apply. How have they done it? What family history, what upbringing, what pattern of individual development contributed to their success? If we are interested in liberating women for self-development, we must try to answer these questions.

Attempts to explain the motivation of women committed to professions dominated by males[10] have been little more than tentative. Alice Rossi, the renowned sociologist, has attributed to these women "extraordinary motivation, thick skins, exceptional ability, and some unusual pattern of socialization."[11] From my own experience with such women, I question profoundly the "thick skins." Indeed, my impression is of enormous sensitivity carefully hidden from view, but paid for by internal torment. What is certainly clear, however, is that such women have an exceptionally strong drive to autonomy. In short, they have become able, by some psychological process, to conceive of themselves as selves.

The word "process" is important in speaking of the motivation of these women toward achievement. Their personal circumstances somehow allowed them to undergo a "process" in which they established a drive toward autonomy. Clearly, most female socialization inhibits such a drive, either plunging the woman into such conflict that resolution appears possible only through retreat, or imposing so much inner tension that the cost of achievement, even where it occurs, is extravagant.

Edmund Wilson has mentioned conflicts women encounter from living "half in a man-controlled world against which they cannot help rebelling and half in a world which they have made for themselves but which they cannot find completely satisfactory."[12] This is a good description of many women, but not quite of achieving women, who do not rebel against the man-controlled world they join, and do not consider themselves part of the world women, any women, have made for themselves.

Women of achievement in so-called male professions are characterized, rather, by their total commitment to the male club they have joined, and their inability to remain women-identified within that club. Sexually women, they are professionally men. They have no wish to rebel against the male world, and no cause for dissatisfaction with the female world they have deserted; it ceases to exist for them. Such women consider themselves exceptional by definition, but definitely within what is for them the inner sanctum, the male world, the place of ultimate belonging.

If it is impossible to uncover a unique pattern or process by which female children evolve into achieving women, one can nevertheless identify several childhood circumstances, one of which, at least, must be present to produce an achieving woman in a male-dominated profession. As will be amplified in the following pages, these circumstances are: 1) socializing forces, perhaps of a particular foreign culture, which encourage professional commitment within a certain class of women; 2) the family position of first-born child, only child, or a child with all siblings very much older or younger; 3) experience in an all-girl environment, either an all-girl family or an all-girl school or college; 4) the role of "son" (not boy) to the father, accompanied by a strong sense of the father as role model; 5) a sense of the mother, however affectionately viewed, as representing a female destiny to be avoided at all costs. (In her recent work, *In Pursuit of Coleridge*, Kathleen Coburn wrote: "One negative consequence of being brought up in a large family in parsonage poverty was the conviction in early adolescence that nothing would induce me to be a parson's wife or the mother of a large family. All that washing and ironing and mending! All that cooking and dusting! Perhaps something was unconsciously conveyed to me of my mother's suppressed craving for a few oases of peace and pleasure.")[13]

Let us look, for a moment, at several women from several countries. At the date of writing (1978) all are living. They have been chosen, if not at random, at least not with the idea of setting a pattern; they serve, however, to indicate connections. They are all, in any worldly terms, successful.

Helene Deutsch. Early woman psychoanalyst with Freud, the woman who encoded his most profound questionings of woman's possibility for healthy achievement outside of the roles of wife and mother. She was born in Poland, of a Jewish family. Her father was sufficiently prominent for his Jewishness to be overlooked. She was born, a fourth child, when her two older sisters were eleven and seven and her brother was ten. The brother had turned out to lack the hoped for "intellect and character." The father, although disappointed at the sex of the fourth child, recognized her "as his spiritual heir."[14] Deutsch wrote of herself that she was in effect an only child, and that Freud later recognized that she considered herself both a girl and a boy, a situation she declined to recognize as meaningful and healthy when she herself wrote about the psychology of women. Her mother "made the normal process of identification with the mother very difficult." (Note the Freudian use of the word *normal*.) "Only now do I realize fully how many of the positive ideals in my life are a reaction against her.

Yet in my heart I have kept to this day a yearning for her love."[15] An extraordinarily moving and accurate statement by the sort of woman who, while achieving exceptional prominence herself, will deny other women the same opportunity without guilt.

Cheryl Crawford. American, theatrical producer, major figure in the Theatre Guild. Her autobiography is entitled, significantly, *One Naked Individual.* She was the oldest child and only girl. She reports[16] that she had to do everything the two next brothers, one and a half and three years younger, did. She did not admire "feminine" girls. Her father was the strong figure, her mother "very feminine with small feet," also described as "gentle and sentimental." The contrast between the two mothers—Crawford's and Deutsch's—indicates two common patterns, perhaps one Jewish and the other gentile. In one, the mother, characterized as a Jewish mother, is a woman of energy and brains whose love must be expressed through a male child, and whose whole life is one of frustration and the manipulation of men, toward whom the daughter feels simultaneously admiration and resentment. The Crawford mother, on the other hand, more the type of the mother of Hennig's women, is treated by the daughter as she is treated by the father: outside the sphere of accomplishment, to be protected and cherished, regarded with affection but without admiration. In both cases, emulation is to be avoided at all costs.

Crawford writes of a time when she was producing Dorothy Thompson's play *Another Sun.* Dorothy Thompson was forty-five:

Dorothy and I often went together after evening rehearsals to a small, ugly bar next to the theatre. We didn't talk much about the play. We talked about ourselves, about being ambitious, independent women. Neither of us felt we had suffered from being women in a man's world—partly, perhaps, because we were just too determined and engrossed to notice. I'm not sure we really cared whose world it was as long as we could pursue our careers. Our consciousness had not been raised. "Women's liberation" was a phrase of the future. Had it existed then, however, I think we would have become part of it.[17]

Helene Deutsch, interviewed in 1972, admitted that women might work, but denied that they might be right, for themselves, in not wanting children: "Oh how sad! Oh, God, how sad! Pregnancy is such a beautiful experience. Something is not quite right if a woman doesn't want a man or a baby."[18] Deutsch was eighty-seven at the time she spoke those words, and Crawford younger. Yet both were speaking in a time of feminism.

If one sets Deutsch's own experience against her recommendations for women, one confronts, in the disparity, the failure of the early women analysts toward women, their inability to imagine as possible for others what they themselves had done. That the only two women analysts of those earlier years who denied the essential Freudian interpretation of female experience, Karen Horney and Clara Thompson, were not Jewish may have some significance. Freud did not represent to them the adored father whose sanction they must have for achievement. One might mention, parenthetically, that according to Deutsch, Freud called his daughter Anna Antigone. One would like to know what he would have made of that identification by another. Perhaps the aspect of Antigone that most attracted him was her devotion to the male members of her family.

Golda Meir. Born in Russia and raised in Milwaukee, she was the second of three daughters. Her older sister, nine years her senior, was her mentor. A revolutionary at fourteen, this sister became the greatest influence on Golda Meir's life—apart from her husband.[19] On the question of "women's liberation" Golda Meir must be quoted at some length.

Do you mean those crazy women who burn their bras and go around all disheveled and hate men? They're crazy. Crazy. But how can one accept such crazy women who think it's a misfortune to get pregnant and a disaster to bring children into the world? And when it's the greatest privilege we women have over men![20]

It is worth pausing a moment to notice the similarity to Deutsch's statements at about the same time. Neither woman was in any sense the conventional mother, but neither could bring herself to admit that, nor to see that unconventional solutions might be essential to other women as well. Deutsch and Meir speak exactly as one would expect a male of their profession and training to do. They cannot imagine other women as themselves. Meir continues, presenting the characteristic account of accomplished women in explaining their success:

When I joined the Zionist labor movement, I found only two other women—ninety percent of my comrades were men. I've lived and worked among men all my life, and yet to me the fact of being a woman has never, never I say, been an obstacle. It's never made me uncomfortable or given me an inferiority complex. Men have been good to me. . . . Of course I've been lucky, of course not all women have had the same experience, but be that as it may, my personal case doesn't prove those crazy women are right. There's only one point on which I agree with them: to be successful, a woman has to be much more capable than a man.

The question arose as to whether Golda Meir regretted leaving home so much, not being with her children all the time:

> No. Because through suffering I gave them a life that's more interesting, less banal than the ordinary. I mean, they didn't grow up in a narrow family environment.[21]

The inability of women such as Meir and Deutsch to think through what they are saying perfectly parallels the failure of the four Harvard women who received the first female Rhodes Scholarships to understand their relationship to other women. It has been said of women—and I shall return to this—that they create themselves, are novelists in the very living of their lives, provide in their explanations to themselves of circumstance the model of the creative mind.[22] Yet the failure of intelligence here is so pronounced that the inability to perceive fact must be recognized as a profound disability of today's women. Meir regrets, in the same interview, how few women are in the Israeli parliament, but she does nothing, has done nothing, to change this. One of the legends that has grown up around Golda Meir is that Ben-Gurion called her "the ablest man in my cabinet." She scorns this, since women are, in her opinion, more able, but misses the entire significance of the tokenism she represents: the occasional woman will be accepted as a man, indeed, if capable, as the best of men.

Indira Gandhi. Born in India, only child of Nehru. Like Meir, she had an unhappy marriage, and devoted more time to her profession of politics than to her two children. (The question of whether "housewives" devote more meaningful time to their children than employed women do must be mentioned, if not examined, at this point.) As Fallaci points out, no man reaching so high a political position would have to consider any conflict with his marriage or parenthood.[23] Listen to Indira Gandhi's answers to Fallaci's questions, the same questions, more or less, asked of Golda Meir: "Have you ever been a feminist, Mrs. Gandhi?"

> No, never, I've never had the need to: I've always been able to do what I wanted. On the other hand, my mother was. She considered the fact of being a woman a great disadvantage. She had her reasons. The reasons, considering the seclusion forced on Indian women, are profound. *Her* mother used to dress her as a man, to allow her to go riding and preserve her sanity.

"What do you think of the liberation movement?" she was asked.

> I think it's good. Good. . . . Women sometimes go too far, it's true. But it's only when you go too far that others listen. That is also something I've learned from experience.

Here is Indira Gandhi's account of her upbringing:

> I grew up like a boy . . . most of the children who came to our house were boys. With boys I climbed trees, ran races, and wrestled. . . . My father cared very much about courage, physical courage as well. He despised those who didn't have it. But he never said to me, "I want you to be courageous." He just smiled with pride every time I did something difficult or won a race with the boys.[24]

Indira Gandhi, like Meir, denies that her children suffered because of her other interests when they were children.

It should be clear that I am here ignoring the political positions of either woman in the direction of her country. What I am searching for is some hint of why one accepts feminism as a fact of life, and the other does not, especially given the probability that Israel has a higher proportion among its citizens of women capable of ruling than does India. Indira Gandhi's sympathy with women's liberation was doubtless influenced by her mother's stories of lost opportunities for selfhood.[25]

From my own experience, which I introduce here in the hope of casting light, Indira Gandhi's ability not to deny feminism as a necessary political movement is also possibly related to her father's experience of Theosophy. When Nehru was a boy, Annie Besant, who followed Blavatsky as head of the Theosophical Society, was lecturing on Theosophy in India. In her audience was the twelve-year-old Nehru, who had for three years studied Theosophy with a tutor.

At the age of thirteen the boy became a member of the Theosophical Society, and was initiated by Mrs. Besant herself. . . . [When the boy later went to England to school] in a remarkably short time Theosophy departed from his life, but he had no doubt that these three years left a deep impression on his thought and character. Though he always retained the warmest admiration for Mrs. Besant, he later lost his esteem for Theosophists in general, feeling that instead of being "the chosen ones they seem to be very ordinary folk, liking security better than risk, a soft job more than a martyr's lot."[26]

In fact, Mrs. Besant returned into the life of Nehru later, and his old admiration for her was renewed.

My father, after his move to New York, also became a student, not of Theosophy, but of what Blavatsky, Annie Besant, and others have called the "Ancient Wisdom." He was later to read the writings of Annie Besant with profound interest, and to study with another woman, Alice Bailey, whose school in New York taught the "Ancient Wisdom." Indeed, my father has said that all the teachers from whom he learned anything lasting have been women. For some years, as a child, I myself studied the "Ancient Wisdom" but abandoned it, partly for Nehru's reasons (the extreme conservatism of those I met in the thirties who devoted themselves to ancient religious ideas was troublesome) but mainly because it led my father—a man of extraordinary intelligence in most matters—into improbable beliefs, such as that Bacon had written Shakespeare's plays, was the son of Elizabeth I, and the reincarnation of Roger Bacon. The last of these claims I did not bother with, but the study of Shakespeare and Elizabeth into which I plunged in my college years proved the absurdity of the first two.[27] I recognized then that a faith that denies facts and scholarship was useless to me.

Yet I am convinced that my father's beliefs permitted him, like Nehru, an attitude toward an only daughter that was far more enlightened than was usual in their place or time. My father's taste in women has always been conventional, yet this in no way interfered with his support of me in my "boyishness," any more than it interfered with Nehru's support of his daughter's "boyishness." Some elements of their religious education were, I think, important here: both men had been taught by women, had studied religions founded by women, and they were not disturbed by envisioning a woman endowed with energy and powerful vitality; also, the theories of the "Ancient Wisdom" included, like those of Hinduism, a belief in reincarnation. Any man who believed himself to have been female in previous incarnations, and destined to be female in later incarnations, was less likely to be terrified by appearances or qualities not strictly applicable to one sex or the other.

Simone de Beauvoir. Born in France, older of two sisters. Although she denied being a feminist even after the publication of *The Second Sex,* she eventually changed her mind, understanding the implications of such a stance. As she was to write, explaining why she concerned herself with the problems of women: "I have an interest in them; and I prefer having taken a limited but real hold upon the world through them to drifting in the universal."[28] Beauvoir's clarity about wanting neither marriage nor children is remarkable: the clarity, that is, not the decision. The decision not to have children and marry sometimes arises out of what Roger Gould has called "an internal prohibition against intimacy."[29] Such was not the case with Beauvoir, who has dared intimacy often, and who is unique among these women discussed here in having a male mentor who was not her father.

Whenever other people made attempts to analyze me, they did so from the standpoint of their own little worlds, and this used to exasperate me. But Sartre always tried to see me as part of my own scheme of things, to understand me in the light of my own set of values and attitudes. . . . For a woman brought up as I had been, it would perhaps be difficult to avoid marriage: but he hadn't a good word to say for it. Whatever happened, I would have to try to preserve what was best in me: my love of personal freedom, my passion for life, my curiosity, my determination to be a writer. Not only did he give me encouragement but he also intended to give me active help in achieving this ambition.[30]

Beauvoir is rare also in her consistent encouragement of younger women. In her realization of women's lack of selfhood she sees women as a "creature intermediate between male and eunuch, which is described as feminine." There has been a certain inclination on the part of other feminists, however, to discount the force of her example because of her lifelong relationship to Sartre. This arises from confusion. Women who cannot, or will not, survive without a man as companion or housemate must not, on that account, be seen as less independent than women who live, for example, with another woman. If dependency needs are involved, they are involved equally in both cases. The woman who lives alone may, it is true, choose that life from strength rather than fear, but she is not necessarily more independent than a woman who prefers a chosen dependency with a man. The essential point is the woman's ability to define herself apart from the man or to believe in her ultimate ability to survive without him.

The response to this declaration is that, whatever claims may be made, the woman is less important to the man than he to her. In his seventies, Sartre lost his vision; Beauvoir came every day to read to him and help him with his work. Had she lost her vision, would he have come to help her in the same way? Certainly there have been a few, rare cases where men have devoted themselves to the accomplishments of women, but seldom when they were of equal stature in the eyes of the world. It may be easier for women to nurture than for men. Yet it does not follow that Beauvoir's relationship to Sartre denies her individuality rather than offering her support. If Sartre was devoid of sexual jealousy, as she was not, he was also able to accept dependence in old age, as she perhaps is not. They have functioned as individuals.

Phyllis Schlafly. In her opposition to ERA, Schlafly helps to provide a nucleus for the radical right. She has opposed feminism in all its forms, in order to enforce women's role as dependent preserver of the male ego. Yet she is a woman of continued public accomplishment who entered law school in her fifties and whose life (as is so often the case with such women) belies the truth of her own advice to others. In the limelight, it is pleasant to pose as womanly, persuading others to stick to the joys of obscure labor.

Schlafly was the older of two daughters and attended a private Catholic school for girls. She graduated from Washington University and did graduate work at Radcliffe. All her political experience (and despite her exaltation of domesticity, she has worked almost all her life) has been in support of right-wing causes. Her husband, an attorney for large oil companies, has always been dedicated to combating communism.[31] It is clear that in her mind, women's rights and leftist causes are connected, if not identical. In this she is probably correct. Certainly her active political career—she ran for Congress when her first child was a year old—has been in support of ultraconservatism. Although there has been a pronounced element of dishonesty in her political career —she has continued, for example, to use arguments against ERA that have been discredited and pointed out to her as false—she has recognized the fact, indeed the necessity, of her allegiance to the male world. Compared to a Helene Deutsch, for example, she emerges as clear-headed in her defense of patriarchal institutions and their necessity to conservatism. Deutsch, while defending Freud's most patriarchal statements about women, herself lived their denial. Both women urge other women to a femininity they themselves have never practiced, both exalt wife and motherhood, but one at least has recognized and openly proclaimed the cause to which she sacrifices her fellow females.

The life of Frances Perkins (1882–1965), an American woman of great accomplishment, is in some ways a paradigm of the female experience of achievement. She was the first woman member of the United States Cabinet. She was profoundly devoted to the amelioration of the unbearable condition of the poor and the working class. The older of two daughters and a graduate of Mt. Holyoke College, she was, from the first, a feminist. Her father, who in her childhood read and enacted Greek plays in the original, began to teach her Greek when she was seven or eight years old. In the words of Perkins's biographer, "within the shadings of affection in a happy family, it was evident that Fanny, as she matured, was becoming more compatible with her father than with her mother or sister."[32]

Her marriage, to a man who soon declined into irreversible mental ill-health, provided her with not only the freedom but the necessity to work. She insisted upon keeping her own name, Perkins, and fought to be so referred to in Mt. Holyoke's alumnae notes, with her professional rather than personal accomplishments. Mt. Holyoke, in fact, ignored her for years, in favor of domestic, volunteer women in a pattern my own experience with Wellesley exactly reproduced. In later years, she fought, unsuccessfully, to prevent the presidency of Mt. Holyoke going to a man. She wrote to a friend: "I don't quite see the sense in conducting a college for one hundred years if it and others like it don't produce at least one female capable of running such an institution." Her statement, however, did not resonate, and Bryn Mawr, almost forty years later, was to repeat the Mt. Holyoke process, even in a time of feminism. Perkins's bravery throughout her life is extraordinary, and she never failed to follow her grandmother's advice to "walk through any doors that are opened."

Yet her suffering as a woman through these years is palpable with strain. She was always to follow the admonition she passed on to her (nonprofessional) daughter: Don't let anyone too close, don't reveal yourself. Roosevelt, as President, asked of her tasks he would not have asked of a man. She felt always that she must not disturb her colleagues' sense of how a woman should properly act. Her sense of other people's dignity and feelings was exactly what one would wish could be the general rule for action in the political world, but her great sensitivity and nurturing qualities were unnoticed and unappreciated and unsupported, except by a very few. It is little wonder that her daughter felt her mother's career admirable but undesirable: Who could choose such strain?[33]

Although she accepted her appointment with the encouragement of women friends who were also feminists, Perkins did nothing, perhaps could not imagine how to do anything, to increase the number of women in government. Sensing that she stood in for all women as Secretary of Labor, she failed to see that her tokenism made the presence of other women in government unnecessary to those in power. In later years, she opposed the Equal Rights Amendment, along with many other politicians, because she feared the loss of protective legislation for women workers, which had been the object of her early political endeavors. The lack of imagination here is notable.

Perkins's end is sadly symbolic. Insufficiently honored in her lifetime, she was at last asked to become a member of an all-male club at Cornell, and to live, as no woman before her had, in an all-male house. She was extremely happy there, in the last years of her long life. At her funeral, eight of the men from this Cornell Club were her pall bearers, and in an act of great tribute, raised her coffin high above their heads as they carried her out. While in the Cabinet, she had agreed, in matters of protocol, to take the position of the *wife* of the Secretary of Labor, so as to offend none of the other Cabinet wives by out-ranking them. As did so many women, she aimed always at the common good. A noble aim—but one ends life carried out upon the shoulders of males, having left no female followers behind.

What part have mothers played in all this? On the whole, mothers have tended to be ultimately ineffective in the formation of achieving daughters. Statistics suggest that the daughters of working mothers have a higher opinion of women generally than do the daughters of homemakers; similarly, girls in a class taught by women will tend to rank women higher on a scale of ability and importance than girls in a class taught by men.[34]

In the past, however, so-called feminist mothers have suffered what might be called the Hedda Gabler complex. Eager to shine in the world, they were unwilling or unable to affront convention or to move out beyond the very strictures of society that confine them. Naturally, the message such women gave their daughters was to be independent, but not so independent that you will endanger social approval or prevent a man from marrying you. The problem for the daughter was that, even if she eventually saw through the dangers of conventional restrictions, she was unable to overcome her fear of denying them. A Southern woman writer has commented that "a girl who began by believing everything her family and teachers said to her, and ended by disbelieving most of these things, [found] that she couldn't keep herself from behaving as if she still believed them."[35]

Naomi Mitchison, in her memories of an Edwardian childhood, recalls that her mother was a feminist, and wanted Naomi to be a doctor. She was sent to the Dragon School in Oxford, one of the few girls in a boys' preparatory school. A writer, she later evinced no interest in feminism nor conflict with the conventional female role. Mitchison's mother, though feminist, was a perfect Hedda Gabler. Utterly devoted to the Empire and ladylike behavior, she would not talk to anyone in trade. She covered Naomi's genitals with a handkerchief when Naomi was a child so that the surgeon, setting her leg, would not see them. She disliked the "commonness" or antics of suffragettes and called herself a *suffragist*. Naomi's older brother, J.B.S. Haldane, was encouraged to be a scientist, even serving their father as his assistant when still a boy. The mother's expressed belief in "feminism," and her desire for Naomi to be a doctor were without noticeable effect.[36]

What have we here, beyond the charms of casual empiricism and condensed biography? Certainly it is suggested that conditions like birth order and maternal and paternal attitudes influence the personality development of girls in ways that affect the probability that they will become committed to a professional career. But one cannot choose one's birth order, nor the family attitudes one is born into. It is, however, important to recognize these factors because it may be possible to learn from them, reproduce them where desirable, alter them where necessary. New patterns of parenting, for example, may help to create conditions in which girl children develop the sense of autonomy and self-reliance that contribute to professional success. Of course, knowledge of these matters is still very limited. Achieving women have been far too little studied, just as, until recently, women in general were far too little studied.[37]

Except during periods of high feminist activity, there has been one positive role model for achieving women: the father. If the father is absent through death, or other cause, and the child is the first born, the mother may serve as the reverse model—this is what I shall *not* become. In that case, there is no positive model of what the girl might be, not even a male one—or there is only the memory of a male ideal. In times of feminism, for example, in the decade of the late sixties to the late seventies, there are some instances of girls undertaking male-dominated professions at the instigations of their mothers. The message comes clear—don't be a nurse or librarian like me; be a doctor. But as far as can be discovered, in times when there is no cultural support for feminism, and these times are many, the mother serves as a role model for achievement so rarely as to be statistically invisible. In such times, woman in her search for "identity," or a self not ultimately defined by a relationship, follows the only model available: the male one.

My friend Tom Driver has described woman's liberation as "the attempt of women to become protagonists in their own stories." He and his wife, Anne Barstow, once asked twelve small groups of women in a workshop to invent stories in which the central character was a woman. Only one group was able to do so. The others told fantasies in which the woman character was rescued or awakened or loved by a man, the true protagonist of their stories.[38]

Woman's fantasies have been trapped eternally in a romance where she is the passive figure, without control, awaiting her destiny in the person of the man who will provide her with a life. Women, like children, have told stories in which the details are more important than the plot, in which their own action is not possible, not imagined.

From fairy tales onward, women's fantasies have been of themselves as the sleeping figure a man will awaken. Yet in stories, as in life, even women can learn to identify with the protagonist, to be, as Denise Levertov was, the quester, not "she who is sought." In stories, as in life, it is the male figure whom society has hitherto allowed to be the protagonist, who must, therefore, for a time, be the model. The possibilities for action which seem inevitably male—as Rich perceived them in her desire for a son—must now be seen as human, possible for women also. Woman must learn to contrive plots in which she is the actor, in which she struggles for control of her own destiny, slays her own dragons. She must learn to look at the male protagonists who have, until now, stood as models for human action, and say: that action includes me. Until now woman has not been part of all that she has met. That was Ulysses, while she, Penelope, waited at home. Woman must now say: I wait no longer.

5

Search for a Model: History and Literature

"Now and then it is possible to observe the moral life in the process of revising itself."[1] The words are Lionel Trilling's; he taught me the process, and its recognition, but would have despaired at the direction I perceived culture to be taking. He understood that what he called the "bitter line of hostility to civilization" runs through modern literature,[2] but he was constitutionally incapable of perceiving the source of that hostility: the revolution of the feminine in life. No more profound revision of the modern life can be contemplated than from this source.

William Gibson has said that in every lucky life there is one teacher who places his finger upon our soul.[3] For me that teacher was Trilling. The irony here—an irony characteristic of women's lives—is that the touch was accidental; Trilling neither intended nor acknowledged it. Most women for whom male teachers become mentors turn to them with a devotion either daughterly or loverlike. I was neither attractive nor submissive enough to have made either role possible, and Trilling had no sense of my discipleship. The word disciple was his, and the role was filled by several men, some of whom became my colleagues and, in interpretations of the process of the moral life, my adversaries. They are the ones whom Trilling confirmed until his death. Yet I think it a more profound tribute to a teacher and writer that he touched the life of someone whose cultural attitudes he could not admire. The opinions of great critics do not terribly matter. What counts for greatness is the ability to perceive the forces at work.

In 1972, the year in which I became, belatedly by any standards, a full professor at Columbia, Trilling, then almost sixty-seven years old, was named the first Jefferson Lecturer in the Humanities by the National Endowment for the Humanities. In an interview with the Columbia undergraduate newspaper on that occasion, Trilling, asked about a merger with Barnard in line with "recent moves toward co-education at Harvard, Dartmouth, Yale, and Princeton," declared: "I'm an old Columbia character. I always preferred to teach boys. I was very old-fashioned about that. I like the old thing of a man's college."[4] Much earlier, when I was a graduate student, and his son, a late-born only child, was still young, Trilling served as an editor of an intellectual book club. I subscribed, reading what he wrote there, as

I read everything he wrote. Once, commenting on children's books, he used the phrase: "If one is lucky enough to be reading to a boy . . ." and there followed all the delightful stories one might then indulge in with one's progeny. I can still feel the pain such a sentence caused me, the desire I then felt, even as he taught me most of what I was to learn about the connection between literary ideas and culture, to let him know that the anger of women, wholly displaced from power, was also a cultural fact.

During all the years we were colleagues he never once talked to me, except in the most routine way of politeness. I used to fantasize that we would one day engage in dialogue—this ponderous phrase exactly explains what I aspired to—and his death, ending all hope for that, released me strangely, not only to frank disagreement with his disciples, my colleagues, but to a realization that the dialogue did not require his presence, could not, indeed, have encompassed it.

By an irony he would have appreciated, I replaced him as a speaker on the night of his death. He, who had given many of his books to the Columbia Library, agreed to deliver the annual address to the Friends of the Columbia Libraries, a group distinguished equally by position and generosity. It was clear, ill as Trilling was, that he would probably not be able to speak on that November night, but no other speaker could be announced because Trilling had not been told of his fatal illness. Someone had to stand by. I was asked as something rather close to a last resort, and I suggested, rather testily I fear, that one of his "disciples" be called in to bat for him instead. This was impossible, perhaps because of their grief. In the end I agreed to substitute in courtesy to those who asked me. My only prayer was that Trilling would not actually die on the day of the dinner. But of course he did. There were commemorative remarks before my turn to speak. Only the brilliance of Gordon Ray turned the mood of the evening sufficiently around to allow for my talk, light in tone, on women and biography. My gentle revenge consisted in talking of women, and, moreover, in ending with a quotation from Trilling that could be used to declare a new dispensation for feminine endeavors. The speech was well-received, and freed me to contemplate my unwilling mentor with the love and disdain the living bear the dead.

Trilling (I never learned to call him Lionel, even in my own thoughts) said of modern literature that "it asks every question that is forbidden in polite society. It asks us if we are content with our marriages, with our family lives, with our professional lives, with our friends."[5] The statement is precisely accurate. What Trilling did not consider is that the "us" in that sentence might be female, and that the hostility to civilization felt by women might lie not in the particularity of that contentment—this marriage, this family, this profession—but in the cultural arrangement of these institutions for females in modern society.

When I say that Trilling did not consider these things, I do not mean that they never occurred to him. Women were beyond consideration in his general statements about moral ideas, except insofar as they impinged upon the lives of men. But he could not help noticing, in certain novels where the discontent of women was treated explicitly, that the subject was, so to speak, around. Trilling saw males as encompassing, in all their actions, the moral condition of society. But not even he could ignore the threat of women to this society set forth in Henry James's *The Bostonians*. It is no accident, therefore, that

Trilling's essay on this novel is the only wildly inaccurate and imperceptive one he ever wrote. "The sacred mothers refusing their commissions and the sacred fathers endangered," he wrote, misreading both James's attitude and the novel.[6] As far as I know, he never took the opportunity to comment on what might be called the feminine revolution without disparaging it, seeing in it profound dangers to the proud, masculine life. He was, of course, correct. The dangers were real. Trilling's greatness lies in his analysis of that masculine life, its civilization he so brilliantly sought to protect and preserve. If I have used that analysis to question the masculine values, to attack and question his paternalism, the creaky courtesy of his patriarchy, I do so in the knowledge that I pay a tribute to him. That he reached and inspired me, who was neither disciple nor flatterer, is a mark of his greatness as a teacher and critic.

I never knew Trilling personally, nor do I know to this day anything about him, probably less than is current on the Columbia grapevine. I never met his wife, though I have read her writings, and I knew of his son's birth only because he was so overjoyed by it—the birth itself and the sex of the child—that his classes (and I sat in all those not limited to College boys) all shared in that exaltation. There was a rumor when I was a student, which I heard even after his death from my own students, that his name was not really Trilling but some more mundane, Jewish name, and that, in line with his aristocratic pretensions, he had changed it to what Fadiman once called the most euphonious name in the critical world. This rumor, nonsense of course, was past squelching. It was the only one I ever heard about him. Like most petty rumors, it was foolish as well as inaccurate: Trilling's Jewishness, his particular background was never, as far as I know, any-

thing but a source of pride to him, as it ought to have
been. He was, I believe, the first Jew given tenure in a
humanities department at Columbia. This occurred, not
alone because of his great talents, but as a reaction to
Hitler and the slaughters in Europe.[7]

He himself stated one of the evidences of his greatness
as a teacher. "It was not honorable, either to the students
or to the authors, to conceal or disguise my relation to
the literature, my commitment to it, my fear of it, my
ambivalence toward it. The literature had to be dealt
with in the terms it announced for itself."[8] His personal
relation to the literature made mine possible. When he
spoke of "the imagination of death and rebirth" he spoke
of Kurtz and Marlow, of young men acquiescing in the
imagination of disaster, not of the rebirth of the feminine
spirit that I dreamed upon, sitting in his classes.

He understood that the transformation of the civilization that had developed until the last third of the nineteenth century was the central theme of modern literature. His affections, however, were with the old
civilization, with community, with the old social relations, and the subordination of individuality to the general good. For many years I too treasured this heritage,
as he had taught me. But I was not, thanks to him, easily
revolutionary or disruptive. Therefore, when the great
issue, as I conceive it, came, I was not only ready to
engage it: I did not underestimate the price of what I
sought to overturn.

Trilling was occupied, one wants almost to say possessed, by the idea of the self. He saw the idea of the self
as that which occupies our literature of the last century
and a half, and he saw that self, moreover, in relation to
culture. He preferred the word "culture" to the word
"society," because, as he said in his marvelously resonat-

ing way, "there is a useful ambiguity which attends the meaning of the word culture." There is a sense in which he saw the self as opposed to culture; indeed, one of his collections of essays is titled *The Opposing Self*. In the introduction to that volume, he describes Yeats's whole career as "his long quarrel with the culture, which, more than anything else, made his passion and his selfhood. Such quarrels with the culture," Trilling goes on to say, "we recognize as the necessity not only of the self but of the culture."[9]

Yet his views on that matter would change over the years, most noticeably over the years in which he and I were at Columbia as members of the same department. In a way far too complicated and too subtle for me to expound here (or perhaps anywhere), Trilling began to shift his sympathies away from the self and toward the culture, as he saw the culture that had produced the Yeatsian self endangered, and as women seemed to place a larger and larger claim upon the culture. Trilling never really conceived the self as properly having its being within a female. Nevertheless, in speaking of the self, and particularly of the "opposing self," he spoke in a way, as I hope to show, particularly meaningful to women.

Greatness for a critic, then, lies in the enunciation of forces: he defines the opposites in dialogue, seeing beyond Diderot and Rameau's nephew and all the other antagonists to the powerful ideas that confront each other in the literature and the culture. If the critic fails, as Trilling failed, to recognize the "anti-hero" (as he liked to call the antagonist of ethical nobility) behind the mask of feminine compliance, his is not a major failure. He left the understanding of their revolution ready for the use of feminists, however firmly he would have disdained their cause. Teaching is a dangerous profession.

That is why universities are feared by dictators and little men dressed in power: because the great teacher can teach *how* to think and interpret, not *what* to think and interpret. So when Trilling, describing Freud, said of him that "he charges women not to interfere with men in the discharge of their cultural duty, not to claim men for love and the family to the detriment of their free activity in the world," we understand, if we are women, our violent exclusion from "free activity," from "men" who make civilization, even from civilization itself. Unlike other thinkers whom he in some ways resembles— Buber, Niebuhr, Tillich—Trilling did not write so that "men," "mankind," etc. seemed to include women in their echo of possibility. When Trilling spoke of men he meant not humanity, but males. He was adamant in his exclusion of women, from his theories as from his college; but if women will read him they will discover the strengths and fears of the civilization they must both infiltrate and overthrow.

It is child's play to translate Trilling's modern quester into a female adventurer; the difficulty lies in persuading women that the dream is indeed for them, that male adventure may indeed be translated into female adventure, the more daring because the more unexpected. When Trilling sets the community against the self, and backs the former, he is backing the male world of power that women ought to understand and accept as adversary. They could find no better teacher, which is what I want to show.

Trilling's last book, *Sincerity and Authenticity,* is particularly useful for this purpose. It is not an original book— almost all his examples have been used by him before— he is refining his thoughts, rather than creating new ones. His originality lies in the earlier books. Here, he has exchanged brilliance for wisdom; he is one of the few critics who rounded off his life in so satisfactory a manner. Certainly, like most old men, he ended despairing of the world that surged around him. Old men should be explorers, Eliot advised, but what they explore is not what youth explores, at least not in Trilling's case. He ended, as great men often end, speaking for the past, urging us to understand it. This final book, however, most clearly indicates the female situation as the modern woman can translate it from its male language, once she has the key. For Trilling both describes the male world and the source of its defeat. When Trilling announces on which ground "a man can set up the smithy in which to forge his autonomous selfhood," a woman must ponder that advice.

Here is Trilling on Rousseau. Rousseau "is concerned to foster a human type whose defining characteristic is autonomy, the will and strength to make strict choice among the elements of our enforced life in society." Trilling urges, with Rousseau, disgust with "the personality whose whole being is attuned to catch the signals sent out by the consensus of his fellows and by the institutional agencies of the culture, to the extent that he is scarcely a self at all, but, rather, a reiterated impersonation." Is there a better description of woman's situation today? Autonomy for women has sometimes been denigrated by those who see no profit in women's imitation of the male scramble for power at the cost of loving. But Trilling's words make clear that the danger is not of imitation of men, but of women's internalization of men's signals and institutions, so that woman appears to preserve herself in preserving man's "signals" and institutions. It is the mark of a caste that it internalizes the judgments of the oppressor, particularly the judgments upon itself.

Tracing the development of the concept of a *self,* which emerges in the seventeenth to eighteenth century, Trilling defines it as that within a person which he "must cherish for its own sake and show to the world for the sake of good faith."[10] Women are only recently taking up autobiography in an attempt to show themselves, and most especially their anger, in compliance with this edict (though the autobiographies are often in the form of novels). Trilling mentions that men, in recognizing selves, live "more and more in private rooms," though it does not occur to him to connect this with Woolf's admonition about private rooms to twentieth century women. Nonetheless, we may listen and learn.

Thinking only of men, Trilling relates Hegel's advice: that Spirit, "if it is to fulfill its own destiny of self-realization, must bring to an end its accord with the external power of society." It must seek "existence on its own account." Rarely has the challenge to women today been more clearly stated. Hegel describes tellingly, so Trilling teaches us, the process by which (women) make the choice to maintain the relationship with society, the prudential reasons why the individual argues herself into the virtues of the external power, in her case, men. This power, Hegel knows, suppresses autonomy. But most tellingly for women, Hegel advises that "the noble self is not shaped by its beneficient intentions towards others; its intention is wholly towards itself."[11] What Hegel saw as essential to the formation of the male self one and a half centuries ago, what Trilling describes to us as essential to an understanding of man's quarrel with civilization, applies now with consummate exactness to the female condition. Women are only beginning to learn about sincerity.

I do not mean to suggest that in reading Trilling women are involved in nothing more than efforts of translation or, perhaps, allegory. It is also necessary to remind oneself, as Trilling praises all that is noble in civilization—"order, peace, honour, and beauty," as well as the family and community—that these values and institutions are maintained at the price of woman's labor. Whenever men long for the honor of a past culture, they fail to mention the cost to that culture of the women who awaited the male return from adventure. One must also watch out for Trilling's "we's." Women are not a part of his "we." When, therefore, he writes that "we reject the archaic noble vision of life because we desire to escape the limiting conditions which it imposes," he does not dream that women may rightfully appropriate to themselves the "we" in that sentence. Trilling, like Werther, is enchanted by "actual scenes of patriarchal life,"[12] and, even where he is defending assertions of self against that life, as he would not do in his later works, he nowhere suggests that the assertive selves might be feminine.

This means, of course, that sincerity may be seen with tolerance, the tolerance of an understanding father for his prodigal son, but when sincerity becomes authenticity—when, that is, it threatens the foundations of Trilling's own world—then self-assertion becomes dangerous. Is it only a coincidence that sincerity transforms itself in Trilling's eyes to something very much less attractive, and more dangerous, when women may be conceived as a part of the challenge?

Jane Austen is the single woman author Trilling ever discusses with admiration, indeed with acclaim for her absolute greatness, even in comparison with Dickens. *Mansfield Park* must, therefore, be the novel that most attracts his interpretation, and indeed his brilliance is

nowhere more evident than in his understanding of this
novel, especially in his perception that charm and goodness are not, as we hope they are, likely to be allied.
Austen was committed, so Trilling claims, to "the ideal
of 'intelligent love' according to which the deepest and
truest relationship between human beings is peda-
gogic."[13] But Trilling nowhere makes clear in what way
the pedagogy leads a woman to selfhood. Did Austen
indeed believe that it did? I doubt this, and I think that
Trilling feared Austen less than he might because he did
not understand (as she did) that for a woman, the peda-
gogic relation, (in which the man is the pedagogue), not
only cannot lead to an "intelligent life," but, in fact,
altogether precludes it. As his earlier comments on
Emma show, Trilling did not believe, or did not believe
that Austen believed, in the woman as a moral force. In
this he was, I think, wrong.

It is not in what he has to say of Austen that Trilling
speaks most meaningfully to women today. The Austen
critic must take note of his remarks, but the woman who
goes to him, as intelligent readers do, for insights into
life and culture must avoid any specific comments of his
on women as women, and listen to the advice he gives,
or records others as giving, to "young men." She must
look especially to his descriptions of the quests and
dreams and desires of young men in search of a self. It
is in these accounts that a woman will learn most of what
she needs to know about the search for sincerity. Its
history is her history, though Trilling never considered
the matter in that light.

Listen, one wants to say to women today, to Trilling's
admonitions to yesterday's young man: "Act out your
own high sense of yourself." Cultivate that aspect of the
self that has for its function the preservation of the self.

And lest we shy away from this cultivation in the belief that it is, especially for women, too egocentric, let us learn from Trilling also that "it is through our conscious certitude of our personal selfhood that we reach the knowledge of others."

Trilling ends his book critical of current ideals, particularly those of existentialism and authenticity. He fears, in a wonderfully bold conclusion, that we aspire to be Christ—but with none of the inconveniences of "undertaking to intercede, of being a sacrifice, of reasoning with rabbis, of making sermons, or having disciples, of going to weddings and to funerals, of beginning something and at a certain point remarking that it is finished."[14] This description, full of all of Trilling's wonderful eloquence, is of a role we must now see women as taking on, even as he feared that men were deserting it. Women's work, we must note, has been without beginnings or endings, and women have been notably lacking in disciples. There can be no question that women's almost total lack of followers—of those who carry on, in an unbroken line, the work of achievement—has been the greatest deprivation in women's history. Above all, however, Trilling, who identified with the rabbis and their patriarchal culture, tells us to reason with the rabbis. We must be willing to be a sacrifice for ourselves, we must intercede. He has told us, however unintentionally, that we, too, partake of divinity.

"The Question was, who was guilty." This sentence, the beginning of Lionel Trilling's story, "Of This Time, Of That Place," is a quotation from Ibsen's *Ghosts*. Trilling has taken a question asked by a woman and of society's degradation of her, and transformed it into a male question, asked in an all-male classroom of a society perceived as having the male at its center. Nonetheless, with characteristic perspicacity, Trilling knew what the question was. I wish to suggest a different answer.

Guilt is an unhappy word. It suggests, reverberates with the profoundest feelings of the human condition, and is, I sense, the question women must ask themselves: after we have recognized the unbelievably hard conditions under which women have struggled throughout recorded history, is there any sense of guilt—I speak of guilt in a Biblical, Greek, Shakespearean sense, with all the implications intact—with which women might discover, as tragic heroes do, the responsibility for our own condition?

All of us who have taught literature must, at some time in our careers, have encountered the student who asks: why was Oedipus to blame? Wasn't he doomed by the oracles? Or, conversely, if he believed that he was to murder his father and marry his mother, why not simply remain a bachelor and avoid anger at all males older than himself? This profound disinclination to confront the tragic question is particularly American. Trilling recognized this, and taught, moreover, that "we fulfill ourselves by choosing what is painful and difficult and necessary."[15] I want, therefore, to explore the ways in which we women (never mind how cruel the circumstances) have betrayed ourselves, and we must realize that whatever the fates ordained, we bear the responsibility and must seek our own enlightenment. The question is not of blame, but of transformation, the transformation, not only of institutions, but of female consciousness as well, the transformation of women from the sufferers in *The Trojan Women* to the heroes in Sophocles's dramas. I want to suggest how a woman might convert the materials of her male-centered education into a guide for female accomplishment.

For what we must realize is that the stories of women are the stories of acceptance, and passivity. To recognize woman's Oedipal guilt for wishing the passivity, the simple "thereness" of the mother, is not to "blame" her, any more than one "blames" Oedipus. It is to suggest that unconscious impulses must be redirected, or at the least, recognized.

Patricia Spacks, in her introduction to a collection of essays, *Contemporary Women Novelists,* mentions that even a cursory survey of fictions about women suggests that they involve "patterns of passivity." "*Martha Quest,* that brilliant study of adolescent rebellion, proceeds, for example, through vignettes of passivity. Martha's determination to make for herself a life different from her mother's leads her to no purposeful, self-ordained action. She exists at the disposal of others."[16]

Speaking of the novels of Jean Rhys, Elgin Mellown recognizes the inevitable approach to the destinies of male and female characters. "The man considers himself to be a free agent in the present moment, not fearing the future and not completely at the mercy of the past. But the woman knows instinctively that she must act out a preordained role and that, no matter what present events may indicate, her end is inevitable."[17] Female authorship, when it has not projected its dreams of action upon male characters, has contrived either to endow the expected female destiny with terror, wit and passion —the romance or the comedy of manners—or shown the inevitable despair of passivity—the realistic novel. As a variation on this theme, women use "motherhood" as an excuse not to succeed outside a domestic role, not to try, or, trying, not to persevere through the necessary pain.

To choose male literary models and reinterpret them to address women is neither a simple nor an exclusive process. That women should not eschew any female model, literary or other, which presents itself is, one hopes, too obvious to need repeated emphasis. Similarly, the complexity of a process whereby women internalize, not men's view of them, nor men's use of them, nor men's ideas of their proper destiny, but that very process by which men themselves have achieved selfhood, is not to be underestimated. The aim of such a process is not imitation of men, except in the Aristotelian sense in which an action is imitated. Least of all is it the adoption of such aspects of male behavior as machismo and fear of the female. These last are the defenses males have adopted in the course of their own difficult path to selfhood. Woman, starting elsewhere, need not even be warned against them.

The major difficulty for women will be to hold in mind at the same moment the male model and its ultimate transformation to female uses. Woman must learn to call whatever she is or does female. For whatever she is or does *is* female. Ultimately, there are no male models, there are only models of selfhood from which woman chooses to learn. In recognizing the maleness of models from the past, woman, at the same time, denies that the connection of these models with maleness is a necessary one. Since woman has been continuously warned to shun the male model, warned that her very being would be endangered were she to follow such a pattern, she needs both to claim the male model and to deny its maleness. There may have been harder tasks, but they would be difficult to name. The hardest in the life of woman is to learn to say: Whatever I am is woman.

The legend of Eros and Psyche is as good a place as

any to begin. Erich Neumann, who subtitled his interpretation of the story, "The Psychic Development of the Feminine,"[18] has (with one or two stereotypical reservations) shown it to be an account of how woman must learn to control her own destiny, to *do* rather than to *be*, if she is to achieve ego stability. Further, Neumann tells us that ego stability in women has been constantly threatened by relatedness—by the need above all to be loved, to be affirmed in one's being only by another's choice to love one. Neumann's interpretation of Eros and Psyche is of great interest because the tendency of male interpreters of the story, artists even more than poets, has been to see it as a tale of feminization, in which the male Cupid is made gentler in a female way, and the two figures, male and female, come to resemble each other to a remarkable degree.

Jean Hagstrum provides the most interesting recent discussion of the process of feminization in Eros and Psyche. He observes, as have so many others (why not women?) that this story, "is rich and complex enough—as all fairy tales are—to justify the many varied interpretations which succeeding centuries have accorded it."[19] Hagstrum's discussion, witty, informative, and illustrated, delightfully presents the interpretation that many feminists have insisted clinches their case against androgyny. Hagstrum shows that in the various representations of the Eros and Psyche legend, it is always the male who is made more feminine, who assumes the virtues of the "feminine" nature. Although Psyche must become slightly more manly to resemble her lover so closely, a glance at the illustrations confirms on the whole the fact that it is the male figure who has been allowed the dual characteristics. Those who criticize the theory of androgyny do so precisely for this reason: the male assumes feminine characteristics, while the female (as in the work of Norman O. Brown) is left with those reproductive characteristics that the male cannot assume, but she takes on nothing of the male character.

Hagstrum recognizes, however, that the qualities in this story, which he interprets as the homoerotic, the narcissistic, and the incestuous, "became very prominent in that breakup of institutions" that marked the spirit of Romanticism.[20] At least the first two of these, the homoerotic and the narcissistic, are also the elements that today's conservatives (Anita Bryant, Phyllis Schlafly, et al.) most fear. The refusal of woman to devote herself exclusively to children and her desire for her fullest orgasmic capacity are condemned by the conservative as narcissistic, while the homoerotic is seen as threatening the family. Implicitly, Hagstrum criticizes those who have attempted to move mankind "toward the liberation of both the sexes from repressing conventions . . . and toward an undifferentiated commonality of men and women." He sees general interpretations of the Eros and Psyche legend as simultaneously endowing males with feminine virtues and profoundly threatening the patriarchal structures of our society.

Erich Neumann's reading of the story he calls "Amor and Psyche," not historical like Hagstrum's, serves much better as an example of the way in which such tales may be adapted by women to a wider and more liberating use. Neumann is remarkably courageous, particularly in 1952, in his interpretation of this myth as indicating the process necessary to women for the achievement of selfhood. He plots the movement of Psyche from the unquestioning lover of a man, her husband, to the awakening of consciousness and the demands not only for her own evolution, but for his acceptance of their separateness, their distinct individualities. The importance of this interpretation lies not only in the necessity for Psyche, the feminine consciousness, to *do* rather than to be, but also in Neumann's realization that women are halted on the road to selfhood by the temptations of pity. The feminine ego, Neumann recognizes, is most seriously threatened by relatedness and its unwillingness to exchange what is at hand for a good that seems abstract. There is some dangerous nonsense in Neumann's rendering of the myth, but considering the date, remarkably little: the danger consists in his identifying the feminine self with beauty rather than knowledge, and in the suggestion that it must stop its growth short of the point reached in masculine development, that is at the stage of beauty and contemplation of the body, which we call narcissism.[21] Neumann's reluctance to allow the female full development of the masculine self, as the male is urged toward cultivation of the feminine self, reflects the enormous bias of those years and of his mentor Jung who, though he understood the importance of the feminine to the masculine, lacked the impulse or imagination to conceive the importance of the masculine to the feminine.

Nonetheless, Neumann's interpretation serves women well. He sees, for example, that Psyche must be persuaded to break the taboo her husband has imposed on her, that she may not see him or know "who he is." "It is the ever-recurring 'Never question me,' the order not to enter the 'closed room,' whose infringement Psyche must encompass." Neumann is outspoken in seeing Psyche's sisters, not, as usually interpreted, as evil, but as a force for liberation, particularly from marriages which "are a symbol of patriarchal slavery," for these sisters have been "given to alien kings to be their handmaidens." Vital to this point is not only the realization that patriarchal marriage is a disastrous institution for both sexes, but also the understanding that the male does not want a mature Psyche, that he will oppose female growth toward full consciousness and that the female must, nonetheless, risk the loss of her lover if she is to enter her destiny. For Psyche is desirable to her lover only when she is living entirely for him, a realization less important for what it tells us of marriage than for what it recognizes as central to the feminine consciousness: the female need for love and relatedness that confirms the male need for power, to the general destructiveness of humanity. Neumann understands that the prevailing situation, with all its advantages for the male, is disturbed by Psyche, that she "dissolves her *participation mystique* with her partner and flings herself and him into the destiny of separation which is consciousness."

Neumann says of Psyche that "with her first three acts she sets in motion the knowledge-bringing masculine-positive forces of her nature. But, in addition, she converted the unconscious forces that had helped her into conscious activity and so liberated her own masculine aspect."[22]

Let us think about *Cinderella*. As Anne Sexton says: "That story."

In Sexton's words:

> The man took another wife who had
>   two daughters, pretty enough
>   but with hearts like blackjacks.
> Cinderella was their maid. . . .
> Her father brought presents home from town,
>   jewels and gowns for the other women,
>   but the twig of a tree for Cinderella.

She planted that twig on her mother's grave
and it grew to a tree where a white dove sat.[23]

Bettelheim, interpreting the same events, writes:

> Since her father gives Cinderella the twig which enhances
> the memory of the mother, it seems to be a sign that he
> approves of her returning from her heavy involvement
> with him to the original unambivalent relation to the
> mother. This diminution of the father's emotional impor-
> tance in Cinderella's life prepares the way for her transfer-
> ring her childish love for him eventually into a mature
> love for the prince.[24]

Analysts, of course, to a man (and woman) see the
universe as revolving around male destiny: attachment
to it, rather than imitation of it, constitutes female destiny. But let us translate those princes who keep awakening and discovering the girls in fairy tales. Suppose—and
what else does one do with fairy tales—that the prince in
Cinderella stood, not for the girl's need to love a man,
transferred in proper Freudian fashion from papa to husband, but for her other self, that "masculine" part of
herself, externalized in the story, to which she must be
awakened to achieve adulthood. So, too, the prince in
Sleeping Beauty. The mother is dead—that is, the early
attachment to the mother must cease, as it must for a
boy. Then, the prince kisses Sleeping Beauty awake, but
not to matrimony and living "happily ever after." No, to
her selfhood, to her ability to live out her own destiny,
to engage, as the boy engages, in the initiation rites that
lead to maturity and rebirth as an adult individual. That
story. Not, as Sexton tells us mockingly, the "happily
ever after" story, the old, lying view of marriage.

One needs to notice, also, that dove, in the tree, which grew from the twig on the mother's grave, who helps Cinderella, just as the animals help Psyche. All interpreters seem agreed that animals who help young women represent in some way their essential animal nature, the ability of women to be in touch with the earth and its creatures. That is so, that is what passes, and should pass, from the nurturing parents to the children before their separation from childhood. The ability to reach that dove, the ants, and the other animals, is what children should take with them into their rebirth at adolescence. It is the best memory of love and should remain always.

Yet, *Cinderella* ends in marriage, which, however much it may be taken as the paradigm of selfhood, even of a woman's uniting with her masculine self, has been for so many centuries the enslaving institution of women. The interpretation of Cinderella's marriage as a unification of self will hardly serve to counter the conventional female dream, still preserved in romances, that a woman's destiny consists in her rescue by a "prince."

Karen Rowe, in a study entitled "Feminism and Fairy Tales," has analyzed the way in which the heroine's role in fairy tales "dooms female protagonists (and readers) to pursue adult potentials in one way only: the heroine dreamily anticipates conformity to those pre-destined roles of wife and mother." Rebellion for such a heroine results only in nagging doubts about her "femininity" and identity. There are few alternate female roles in fairy tales, and the female reader is subtly warned against "unilateral actions by aggressive, self-motivated women," like Cinderella's stepsisters, or all stepmothers; fairy tales join the conventional culture in "transmitting clear warnings to rebellious females." Yet Rowe recognizes how strong is women's resistance to rebellion against the stereotype of the waiting, passive woman in fairy tale and romance: "the female psyche has not matured with sufficient strength to sustain a radical assault upon the patriarchal structure." For there are, as yet, too few contrary models to catch the imagination of the young woman, or girl. Rowe concludes her sad analysis with the hope that woman's new psychic and cultural experience will "grow fairy tales for human beings of the future,"[25] tales that will break the cycle of female commitment to passivity and fear of aggression.

Here one feels particularly the importance of not limiting the female imagination to female models. Bettelheim has shown how small boys can use the female model of helplessness in fairy tales to reduce their anxieties and unmentionable fears; similarly, young girls should be able to use male models to enhance their feelings of daring and adventure. To choose only the most obvious example, consider the many Grimm fairy tales employing the theme of the "three brothers." What if the girl could conceive of herself as the youngest of the three? Powerless, scorned, the one from whom least is expected, even by himself, this third brother, because of virtues clearly "feminine"—animal-loving, kind, generous, affectionate, warm to the possibilities of affiliation— this third brother, again and again rejected, nonetheless persists to success with the help of his unlikely friends, and despite the enmity of what, in the person of the two older brothers, might be called the "male" establishment.

Five of the Grimm fairy tales can serve as examples: "The Golden Bird," "The Queen Bee," "The Three Feathers," "The Golden Goose," and "The Water of Life." In all the stories, the two older brothers despise

the youngest, who is usually called Simpleton or Dumml-
ing, and are quite willing, when threatened, to deprive
him of everything or even to kill him. In spite of this
intention the youngest will rescue his brothers when they
have become entrapped by their own selfishness. In
these stories, even though the third brother has proved
himself once, the older brothers convince the father that
he is inherently inept, and he is forced to prove himself
several times over—a paradigm of female experience in
the male power structure that no woman with aspirations
above that of sleeping princess will fail to recognize.

The third brother has, interestingly for the purposes
of the women whose model he will be, internalized others' opinions of himself: he does not doubt his own in-
adequacy. In one story, "The Golden Goose," even his
mother scorns him and feeds him less well than his
brothers; one might recall here the experience of Yezierska's heroine in *Bread Givers,* when the woman in the
cafeteria tries to give her less food than the men although she works as hard and is as hungry. The third
brother, in short, lacks that cluster of characteristics we
have come to label "masculinity." Unlike Cinderella or
even Psyche, however, he uses his "feminine" characteristics of nurturance and relatedness to help him on the
path toward selfhood. Although he is almost always rescued or helped, he does not await help as if it were his
destiny and he does not expect it. His dependence on
help is characterized not by his expectations of rescue,
but by his openness toward others and before experience. Unlike his brothers, he does not presume to know
the value of everything in advance of experiencing it. But
while embodying the "feminine" virtues, the third
brother moves, quests, acts, performs; he is not passive,
he does not wait. Combining the stereotypical "mascu-

line" and "feminine" qualities, he is not committed to those in power, by whom he is considered superfluous, inessential, not of inherent value. In the fairy tales, the power structure is wrong.

One of the stories, "The Water of Life," provides a model not only for the girl aspiring to selfhood, but for her likely experiences as a token woman. In this tale the third brother is accepted only so long as he does not challenge the older brothers' power. So the woman will be accepted, so long as she does not become supportive of other women, nor challenge the male view of how things should be run. Though she rescues her male peers from dragons, they will not be grateful, nor perhaps even tolerant.

Bettelheim, in *The Uses of Enchantment,* is typical in his male use of female figures. Boys may project themselves onto a female figure like the Goose Girl where it is useful.[26] Martin Green, to take a contemporary critic, may say "I am Lady Chatterley," as Flaubert could claim to be Emma Bovary, but women here, as elsewhere, have denied themselves, as well as been denied, the use of male figures as surrogates for their own experience. Yet much of modern critical theory (to go no further) supports such a use. Take, for example, Propp's formalist analysis of fairy tales into seven "spheres of action":

1. the villain
2. the donor (provider)
3. the helper
4. the princess (a sought-for person) and her father
5. the dispatcher
6. the hero (seeker or victim)
7. the false hero[27]

One character may, of course, play more than one of these roles. But notice that only the "sought-for person" is identified by gender. Other figures may be female, but only the princess *must* be. What woman must learn to assume is that she is not confined to the role of the princess; that the hero, who wakens Sleeping Beauty with a kiss, is that part of herself that awakens conventional girlhood to the possibility of life and action.

Structuralism supports this admonition to ignore the marked gender in the characters of myths and fairy tales. In "The Sex of the Heavenly Bodies," for example, Lévi-Strauss shows how the sex of the moon and sun are by no means constant from culture to culture, or language to language, or even always within one culture. Nor is there anything in his theories that insists upon the sex of the constituent parts. Men now trade women exogamously, but the structures themselves do not require this; the structures would work identically if women traded men. The point is that the structures are human, not sexually dictated. This is what woman must learn. As Margaret Fuller said, "Jove sprang from Rhea, Pallas from Jove. So let it be."[28]

Female use of the male model need not, however, remain a matter of translation. Sometimes myth, tale, and tragedy must be transformed by bold acts of reinterpretation in order to enter the experience of the emerging female self. We are, in fact, all aware of such a process, though not used by women. When Freud named the central event in his model of human development the Oedipus complex, he did not, of course, exhaust the possibilities in that play by recognizing its uses for his purpose. Much of the play, indeed, all those elements that we who return to it again and again for its tragic catharsis most celebrate, was ignored by Freud. In much the same light I wish to suggest how another Greek tragedy might be transposed for my purposes. Difficult as this exercise is, I undertake it in order to show concretely the sort of reinterpretation I now urge upon women.

Male myths *about* women, interpreting women for male purposes, have, of course, predominated. Woman, if she has not already internalized these myths, twists and turns in pain, searching for herself within their narrow confines. As Sandra Gilbert suggests, the female poet "writes in the hope of discovering or defining a self, a certainty, a tradition." Women poets, considering and discarding available metaphors, strain "to formulate an ontology of selfhood." Few women poets have managed a complete self-definition, Gilbert points out[29] because they lack models of female selfhood but are, nonetheless, excluded from the use of male models.

But why this exclusion? Femininity, apparently, has been so fundamental that women cannot hope to eschew or evade it, at the same time that it is so superficial that any enactment of a "male" role fatally threatens it. Women have become convinced that if they step outside of the narrowest boundaries of accepted behavior, they will be deprived of what is so biologically fundamental that it must determine their destiny.

Women may begin by knowing they are Hamlet, not Ophelia, Lear as well as Cordelia: certainly the fool. The howl of old age is not alone a masculine howl. Above all, one is not Miranda (a male fantasy), not even Ariel, but Prospero. One has evaded one's duty to the state, been set adrift in a small vessel with one's child, but one knows one's power, one's fault in having eschewed responsibility, and one returns to rule. All this is easier than transformation in those stories where the very action itself occurs between the sexes, and where the woman's natural instincts go to the woman character. That is where great imagination is required, where, indeed, scoffers, who will have an easy enough time of it, risk little by ridicule. I am willing to risk that ridicule, for without risk, we will have nothing, and derision has only the power we give it.

Let us look, then, at that very tragedy, or group of tragedies, that feminists believe reveals the moment of the patriarchal takeover, and the deprivation of female right: the *Oresteia.* I do not mean here to renounce the feminist interpretation; indeed, such a task would be both foolish and unscholarly. Nor, in using the work of a scholar such as Froma Zeitlin, who argues that the *Oresteia* demonstrates "the dynamics of misogyny,"[30] do I mean to imply, either that I consider Zeitlin's interpretation wrong, or, on the other hand, that she would agree with a syllable I write here. I want merely to suggest how women, like men, may use the dynamics offered them from male experience.

To come to the point at once, I shall argue in what follows that Orestes himself can be conceived as providing the paradigm for female achievement of the self. Let us first notice, however, that the entire play is surrounded by female forces, not all of them by any means traditional, stereotypical, or previously portrayed in myth or epic or on the stage. First, we have Clytemnestra, a woman who has taken over certain aspects of behavior characterized as "male," who speaks of herself as "mere woman" with what Lattimore calls "massive sarcasm." She appears to have stepped from woman's sphere into man's. The question the play will ask, among others, is: Has she done so successfully? Was that, indeed, her aim? At the end of the trilogy we encounter Athene, a rare female creature, vastly misunderstood and misrepresented, not least by certain women classicists. With her are also the female deities, the Erinyes, or Furies, who, at the end of the last play, are transformed and raised to a higher place in the hierarchy of the gods. Finally, there is Electra, Orestes's sister, and the only woman in mythology who conspires in the murder of her mother. The poets invented her; she is not in the tradition.

The *Oresteia* has been seen, of course, as the great mysogynist tragedy. The solution of the struggle is seen as male above female on the social and political level. Certainly such an interpretation is historically accurate and need not be refuted. The greatness of a work of literature lies precisely in the degree to which its interpretations ramify. To put this another way, the structure of profound societal change is enacted in the play; whether the change goes one way or another may be determined by whether we see the work historically or metaphorically. Both interpretations aspire to correctness, and at different times, or even simultaneously, achieve it.

In the opening play, the *Agamemnon,* Agamemnon returns from the Trojan War to be greeted by his wife, Clytemnestra, who, together with her lover Aegisthus, Agamemnon's traditional family enemy, will murder him. Clytemnestra has three clear motives for the murder: Agamemnon has sacrificed her daughter, Iphigenia; he has brought home a concubine, Cassandra; finally, in Aegisthus, Clytemnestra has found another lover who does not desert her for ten years at a time. Agamemnon returns pompous and swollen with vanity; Clytemnestra kills him.

We are left, then, at the end of the first play, with a wife having exceeded "wifely" rights and powers and overthrown her husband. She, in turn, is then overthrown. The question for purposes of this feminist interpretation is: May we not regard the overthrow of Clytemnestra by Orestes and Electra, and its defense by Athene and Apollo, as the symbolic moment when the institution of motherhood is overthrown? Motherhood is that institution in which woman has long been enslaved, which has doomed her children of both sexes to endless fears and fancies. Clytemnestra, a strong and willful woman, like many women, has turned and twisted within the role of wife and mother, but found that individual selfhood is not attainable there.

Clytemnestra has, inevitably, been called masculine by many thoughtless critics. The truth is rather as Kuhns describes it: "The control she gains for Argos is achieved through treachery, adultery and terror."[31] These are the only means available to competent women imprisoned within the walls of "motherhood."

Feminists will object that for a woman to suggest the "murder" of a mother, however symbolic, is to join with the worst male forces, including those who destroyed Clytemnestra and established male rule thereafter. But it is not a woman who is being symbolically murdered: it is the principle of motherhood. That principle, not its action in loving parenthood, but its establishment as an institution, must be demythologized and ritually destroyed. Orestes's and Electra's fear of mother-engulfment, which prevented their achievement of selfhood and individuality, is today still a real fear for both sexes, but especially for women who have been institutionalized into a role where rebirth, initiation, and selfhood are impossible.

Let us, at the same time, recognize that although Electra understands the forces that stand between her and selfhood, she is unable to act upon that knowledge. Instead, she awaits the arrival of Orestes to bring about her salvation and confines herself to helping him once he has appeared. Unlike Electra, women must be ready to forego this waiting for the male, brother or other, to be the rescuer, the savior. Electra must learn to become her *own* brother, to become, in short, Orestes.

The truth about Clytemnestra, of course, is that she is not an "independent" woman in any sense of the word. She has responded as women without power do respond, seeking domination and revenge, often unconsciously, as in the powerful Portnoy mother. It is possible, I think, to see Orestes's or Electra's act as that of any individual freeing himself or herself from the female dominator who will not overturn the rule of men but who subverts them and, in the process, her own children of either sex.

This brings us to Athene. Athene has had a very poor press, among feminists and womanly women alike. Pomeroy, for example, calls her "the archetype of the masculine woman who finds success in what is essentially a man's world by denying her own femininity and sexuality."[32] It is significant that Pomeroy's footnote refers to Helene Deutsch in this connection. So we continue in circles, having called all achieving women masculine, we insist upon seeing them thus. But Athene, the goddess, has no more denied her femininity than have those modern, mortal women in any job or profession who have shown themselves capable of achievement.

In destroying their mother, Orestes and Electra freed themselves for their own selfhood, for their initiation rites. If I interpret this as the overthrow of motherhood, it will be claimed that such an overthrow will destroy woman's joy in childbirth, will prevent her spending a period of her life with her small children, etc. The fear is absolutely fundamental. It is not an accident that the most conservative political and intellectual forces in our culture have rallied around the family as the last bulwark against sweeping social change. It *is* the last bulwark. Furthermore, the vision of a world without a mother devoted entirely to one's infant self is dreadfully threatening, almost as threatening as that of the mother reengulfing one's no longer infant self, which forces the male into antifemale stances and the female into total dependence upon a male, fatherlike figure.

At the end of the *Oresteia* is created a marriage that requires, as Zeitlin puts it, "the primacy of the father-son bond in patrilineal succession."[33] The father-son bond, the passing of power to one of the (same) male sex, is of course responsible for the anomalous position of females today, including the absence of any role model for a woman of purpose other than her father. What Orestes is perhaps responding to, however, is that myth which still gripped the Greek imagination even at the time of the *Oresteia:* the mother-daughter bond. The mother (Demeter) held power, which she would use in her anger at the rape of her daughter (Persephone). Certainly there is an echo of this mythical power in Clytemnestra's fury at the destruction of her daughter, Iphigenia. Orestes substitutes one parent-child bond for another.

What the female Orestes must establish today is an institution of marriage and the family in which the parent-child bond is profound until such time as the child undergoes initiation rites into selfhood, but is not inevitably established with one parent or the other simply because of gender. In murdering motherhood, the female Orestes strives to establish with the help of Athene and the Eumenides a political situation in which power is vested in neither sex.

The Eumenides, who have been the Erinyes, can, like Athene, be seen as extending rather than diminishing true female rights. The Erinyes, or Angry Ones, traditionally avenged the killing of one's kin and especially, as in this case, one's mother. In the play, they object because Orestes does not suffer for the murder of his mother as he would have suffered for the murder of his father. In the conventional interpretation (within, of course, the framework of Greek history and belief) it is always because Orestes is *not* made to suffer, that mother-right is here thought to be abrogated and the right of the male line established. But it is possible, if one chooses to interpret the play in a contemporary light— as do novelists and playwrights who adapt Greek dramas and myths for their own purposes—to see the transformation of the Erinyes into the Eumenides as the acquiescence of the female spirits in the destruction of motherhood and as the affirmation of self-creation, of the passage of initiation rites by our female Orestes, by Orestes, that is, speaking for woman now. Let me repeat: I do not mean that this is what the play said to the Greeks. I suggest that we have here a myth, or story, in which the action of woman, here portrayed by Orestes and Electra, can be seen completing the process that will allow their selfhood. The spirits that have always defended the old marriage bond, the old institution of motherhood, here reconstruct themselves into that modern spirit of nurturance in men and women that is not destructive of the earth and its riches, but which recognizes a new order of individuals. They have "the rich earth in their keeping."[34]

As Kitto points out, the Eumenides will try to prevent, not strife between kin, but strife within the state and, by implication, between states.[35] In short, there is a recognition in this play that the institution of "motherhood" as enshrined is no longer a benefit to the earth, and though many (like Clytemnestra) will try to defend it and demand vengeance upon those who fight motherhood, in fact the Furies are transformed into the defenders of a new order, where individuals are more kindly and institutions of kinship less inevitable. As Zeitlin says of Orestes (not of course, in support of this theory), his "salvation is contingent upon his successful separation from his mother." The Erinyes, Zeitlin continues, are "representatives of a negative matriarchy that must be overcome." Though she, of course, sees this matriarchy as negative in male eyes, I suggest that, in the contemporary interpretation, it represents the institution of "motherhood," fatal to female self-creation. Athene, let it be emphasized, must not be seen through Deutsch's Freudian spectacles as "mannish," denying her femininity. On the contrary, she denies the institution of motherhood, but still retains the nurturing behavior usually associated exclusively with women. As Zeitlin says of her, "Female born of male, she can ally herself with male interests and still display positive nurturant behavior."[36] Zeitlin calls her the "androgynous compromise," and indeed she may stand as the answer to those who fear androgyny serves only male interests. Athene is, in fact, a woman who has acquired desirable male characteristics. She will be condemned as denying her womanhood only by those unable to free themselves from stereotypical forms.

To call for the overthrow of motherhood is profoundly revolutionary, and surely invites angry and sarcastic counterattack. Is there a point in stating that one is not urging the relegation of infants to institutions, nor the decline of parenthood? The purpose of "overthrowing motherhood" is to return the father to home and family and to the active care of his infant children, while relieving the mother of the full-time care that his absence has enforced. The other side of abortion is the transformation of each child into a desired child.

The sense of Aeschylus's characters that the father is the true parent and the mother only an incubator must be seen in its positive, metaphoric sense. The man-centered woman has always literally followed the Greek concept: Constance Chatterley says of her pregnancy: "It is to have him [Mellors] inside me." This is the true patriarchal view. But reading the claims of the play metaphorically, for the salvation of the She-Orestes, we can see that the acceptance of the mother as an incubator denies her, quite properly, sole parenthood, sole qualification for the care of the child. That the fetus develops in her body would not, in that interpretation, mean that she alone, or her woman surrogate, should nurture it afterward. This view emphasizes the father's parenthood in a way we must celebrate: sharing in the child's creation, each parent—father as well as mother—must share parental responsibility. The mother's body is the incubator, the seed is from both, and both must be concerned after the child's birth. She-Orestes, in establishing paternal investment in the child, establishes also the necessity of paternal as well as maternal care. "Motherhood," alone is not sufficient.

In a patriarchal society, males must control the production of children; that is why conservatives like Schlafly, Orthodox Jews, the Roman Catholic hierarchy, and the John Birch Society oppose abortion. They defend not the right to life but male control of childbirth. The institution of motherhood, properly sanctified, is the expression of that control; the woman's womb is reserved for paternal purposes. In destroying "motherhood," woman frees herself to be a mother, most often in consultation with a father, but not necessarily, and not in opposition to her own wishes. Thus the commitment of She-Orestes to motherhood's destruction.

There is more to female devotion than the word "motherhood" comprehends. The myth of Demeter and Persephone is about the bonding between women that can be their salvation in a world where they have their fair share of power. It is the only such myth I know, and it is not about "motherhood" but about the sturdy loyalty and application of power that the older woman can use on behalf of a younger one. Demeter has often been called an "earth mother" by men, but was no such thing: she was the goddess of the fruits of the "civilized cultured earth."[37] Altogether noble and womanly, Jane Harrison tells us, she was "perhaps not what the modern mind holds to be feminine," belonging to a time before goddesses became "abject and amorous."[38]

She shared power equally with her brothers, Zeus and Hades, and when Hades attempted to "takeover" a younger woman companion (whether or not her daughter), she fought with the power that was hers as an autonomous god. The result was a compromise: Persephone (or Kore) spent a third of the year in the male domain, during which time the earth was barren. For the rest of the year she was the companion of the older woman, and the earth flourished. That women have power, and might use it in support of one another and to make fair bargains with the patriarchal world, is an idea few women have imagined, few acted upon. They have let men tell them who they are and what they are entitled to.

In the name of motherhood, woman's rights over her

own body and her own destiny have always been denied; beyond this, woman herself has, at the height of every feminist revolution, retreated from a position of strength lest "motherhood" be threatened. Linda Gordon's history of birth control in America carefully documents this fact. Gordon sees birth control as not a single issue, but inevitably connected to women's political rights generally. In her view, the profound misogyny of Christianity and Judaism was in danger of driving women from religion altogether, unless they were offered a promise of redemption: that redemption was motherhood. To the biological and social components of motherhood was added an ideological one. This ideological vision of motherhood, which must be dissolved if female autonomy is to be achieved, demanded that the biological and social components of motherhood be conceived of as indivisible and not be threatened by any female autonomy whatever. It was always opposed to the genuine pleasures of mothering. "Like many forms of repression," Gordon writes, motherhood "was overdetermined." It had, that is, several social functions each of which alone might have been enough to support it. Indeed, this form of repression received almost universal assent. It was approved by liberals as well as by conservatives; it bore not only the good-housekeeping seal of approval but finally the intellectual seal as well, conferred on it by the high priest of the avant-garde, Dr. Freud. All joined in defending an indispensable bastion of male autonomy. But even as they demolished the feminine mystique, women must now join in dismantling what Gordon calls the motherhood mystique.[39] Its useful parts can be reassembled elsewhere.

Need we conceive of the murder of motherhood in action as violent as that of the *Oresteia?* I believe so. It is not accidental that the Greeks have provided us with the form for essential human revolutions. Because women turn now from the longest servitude on record, they must seek for models of action in literary or dramatic figures probably not female. I regard Orestes in this light, without, of course, suggesting that the Greeks would have countenanced, let alone intended, any such interpretation. As women, we must recreate masterpieces. We must use myth "in a setting of contemporary political institutions." As Kuhns has suggested, speaking of course only of the situation in the Athens of Aeschylus, Orestes's "exile has prepared him for the role of the mortal through whom the moral enlightenment is to take place."[40] So woman's exile from the center of action has prepared her.

Thomson tells us that "the matricide is acquitted by an appeal to historical expediency, and the trilogy ends with the ratification of a new social contract, which is just because it is democratic."[41] We perceive the democratic differently now, if we are women. And the matricide is not of a mother, but of an institution.

The same male powers that fight for the preservation of motherhood fear the dissolution of the marriage bond, which will lead to sexual independence and "be manifested politically by a desire to rule."[42] This "fear" is surely justified, but must be seen as fears so often are, as a possibility, including risk. (That marriage as an institution seems unlikely to survive in its present form will be discussed below.)

Orestes, in the Greek version, murdered motherhood to destroy what he feared would be female domination. A female Orestes today must undergo the same rite, this time to establish marriage as an equal partnership and to assure an equal possibility for political power. To do this, however, the female Orestes and Electra must, like their Greek counterparts, destroy the maternal principle —but not the parental one, whether male or female— thus ensuring their own rebirth. The male destruction of the mother must now be reenacted by the female, not for the assumption of dominance, but rather for the sake of equality.

Muses are for men. From Homer ("Sing in me, Muse, and through me tell the story") through Sidney ("Fool said my muse to me, look in your heart and write") to Robert Graves ("Woman is not a poet: she is either Muse or nothing") the muse has been progressively seen as male property and male inspiration. The question of who is woman's muse, and what that muse's sex has not been asked until recently. Graves, indeed, is typical of his age in suspecting that women poets may be seeking a foothold on male inspiration. If woman *is* to be a poet, Graves says, and he finally grants that she *may* be, she must not claim even the status of "honorary man;" he conceives her as even less than a token woman: her destiny is to be inevitably "loving, serene, wise."[43]

What then of women poets? The question is not an easy one and has been rarely confronted. Margaret Fuller, recognizing that woman had a choice between being the muse for men or Minerva for herself (Athene, that is, she of the *Oresteia*), counseled women to be Minerva, eschewing the role of Muse.[44] But there, until recent years, the matter rested. It is, of course, immensely important for the woman to identify her muse, because without a muse, she may be without inspiration, or the personification of her own greatest powers.

Is it a matter of simple reversal: a woman's muse must be masculine? To avoid confusion in answering this question, we must take care to distinguish muse from that other Greek word, *mentor*. Mentor, a friend of Odysseus, was entrusted with the education of Telemachus, and the word has come down to us, through the Latin, connoting now something more than a mere teacher, in fact, a guide or exemplar in dealing with the central concerns of one's life. In discussing the woman's muse, it can be a source of great confusion that male mentors have played a crucial role in the lives of most female artists and, indeed, most accomplished women.

It is no accident that those women who became painters and sculptors until very recently had fathers who were painters or sculptors, or brothers or, more rarely, friends. Without male support, instruction, and sponsorship, female artistic accomplishment was difficult, at one time impossible. Mary Cassatt, whose work was always conceived in her lifetime by her family and many others as an inadequate substitute for marriage and children, had Degas as her mentor. Typically, therefore, Nancy Hale, in her biography of Cassatt, refers to Degas as her muse. "A woman's muse must, by psychological logic, be male, be Apollo. Mary Cassatt's muse was to find its mortal tenement in many 'strong influences,' but principally in Degas."[45]

We have by now learned that the simple reversal of patterns will not do. Sidney's direction from his muse, "Look into your heart and write," is less simple for those who suspect, or know, that what they find in their hearts will not be sanctioned by the males in power. In the artistic world, as in the academic, the point of view that women commit themselves to with complete conviction is likely to be labeled by the dominant men as "trivial," or insubstantial. It is placed, by assumption, outside the mainstream, the major discipline, and allowed to continue, if at all, only along the minor channels and canals that constitute the tributary waterways.

Emily Dickinson, now recognized as a profoundly important figure in American literature, presents perhaps the most powerful vision of the woman poet's dialogue between herself and her muse. One must, of course, begin by realizing that Emily Dickinson was not, as she was for so many years conceived to be, a timid, girlish figure (MacLeish called her a "girl" after her death at the age of fifty-five) but was, as in Adrienne Rich's words, "a practical woman exercising her gift as she had to, making choices." She lived, Rich declares, a life deliberately organized on her terms. "She was determined to survive, to use her powers, to practice necessary economies."

About her life we may at last understand that her seclusion arose not from fear or timidity, but from her insistence upon controlling those circumstances that permitted her poetry. "The real question," Rich has written, "given that the art of poetry is the art of transformation, is how this woman's mind and imagination may have used the masculine element in the world at large, or those elements personified as masculine."[46]

The male poet, endowed by society with "those elements personified as masculine," is free to call upon the "feminine" within himself, or those elements personified as feminine. But in calling upon those elements personified as masculine, a woman risks her identity as a woman, her "femininity." Because "femininity" has always been conceived as a relationship to men, whether as sex object, mother, or wife, it can be unbearably threatened by the use of what are termed "male" powers. It is perhaps for this reason that women poets have tended to personify their inspiration as male, as a lover or master, or both. Only if their "masculine" powers are conceived of as dominating them in an acceptable way can the threat of their poetic powers to their "femininity" be borne.

Rich has recognized that "a woman's poetry about her relationship to her daemon—her own active, creative power,"[47] has had to use the language of male love or male mastery. But Dickinson, Rich believes, understood this, or at least expressed it in her writing. Her life and poetry convey an understanding that the woman poet's daemon will seem destructive, but that once recognized, the daemon cannot be ignored.

It is no accident that for years scholars searched for, took for granted, Dickinson's lost lover. How else explain her seclusion, and her poetic mention of men, or a masculine God, as threatening her with absolute illumination? But if we see, as Rich has taught us to see, that Dickinson embodied her own creative powers in a masculine personification, the search for the literal lover or God becomes foolish, misguided.

If, however, we accept that nineteenth century women such as Dickinson struggled with the terrible conflict of having to sacrifice their "womanly" selves for their "manly" powers, is it inaccurate to say a woman's muse is masculine? The answer is that, unless one is a genius like Dickinson, the struggle within the woman poet against a "male" muse will, because of the world's judgment of what is "feminine," take place at too high a cost. Poetry must cost great women poets no more than it costs great men poets; perhaps, because of the long years of silence, it may for a time cost less.

The woman poet, then, must be enabled to perceive her muse as of whatever sex, but not threatening her social being. This will become possible only when the social concept of "femininity" is abandoned, so that any-

thing a woman does is female: nothing is alien to her, if
she does it; as Dickinson has written:

> Adventure most unto itself
> The Soul condemned to be—
> Attended by a single Hound
> Its own identity.

This means, of course, that women must abandon the
fantasy of womanhood, that fantasy provided by fairy
tales and romances, and perceive themselves as the active principle: in short, as whole, with integrity. Iris Murdoch has said that freedom from fantasy is the beginning
of human liberation.[48] It is certainly the beginning of
poetic liberation.

Historical studies of nineteenth century women poets
suggest that they confounded the lover and the mentor
into an inspiration it was necessary both to welcome and
resist. "Finding themselves heirs to a long succession of
fathers, these women share the vision of a father lover
that surpasses individuals."[49] Not a bad image of a muse,
sexes reversed, except that the man, in turning to the
muse, turned to what seduces, and the woman turns to
what rapes.

Male poets, at least before Freud, when they thought
of God as blessing them, redeeming them from sin, used
the imagery of rape: for example, Donne's "except you
ravish me." But for a woman to think of herself as rav-
ished by her muse, even if he is confounded with her
God, is to suggest to herself a passivity and fear not
healthy, as it may be for a man, but full of terrors for the
self. Such a vision also persuades the woman poet that
her poems derive, in far too literal a way, from something
not herself.

Male poets, Feit Diehl believes, retain the power to separate their "poetic fathers" from the muse: perhaps because they are different sexes. For the woman poet, the confusion between the male mentor, or precursor, and the muse seems to demand of her too great passivity. There is a pull of "attraction and terror."[50] The male muse is both feared and desired, and the woman poet is placed in the position of the heroine of Gothic romances: the villain turns out to be the hero after all, and she both hopes and fears to be overwhelmed.

The truth of this pattern is, however, a nineteenth century truth, and must be recognized as such. When the woman's muse is no longer seen as either Pan or male mentor, but as daemon, no more "male" than Sidney's muse is "female," both belonging to the poets themselves, then the terror with which the female poet faces the muse will be poetic, not social, terror. For the terror arises from the social cost to woman of losing her timidity, passivity, "femininity"; once the cost of creation is faced, or diminished, the terror of the woman's muse, however personified, will be no greater than the male poets' terror of his muse, which was often great, as it must be.

Women must be released from the inevitable bind of their femininity. On the one hand, femininity is bedrock, biologically determined; it must prevent their high accomplishment in previously male spheres. On the other hand, it is so frail, so likely to be crushed by any impulse of action or assertion, that it must be guarded assiduously. Both statements cannot be true. It is even possible that both are false. In any case, woman must not continue to be placed in fear of losing what she cannot escape.

It is well to remember that the muses, as a mythological group, had in their keeping the various genre of artistic achievement and were not conceived as the particular inspiration for individual poets. When Homer began the *Odyssey* with the words "Sing in me, O muse" he called upon the muse of epic in the sort of metaphor common to that time and that art. The *Oxford Classical Dictionary* tells us that the muses "have few myths of their own." They represent the various modes within which artists may aspire to expression and to glory. That men have captured muses for their own is simply another example of male imperialism. A muse may be of any sex, and probably has been, for men and for women. The *Classical Dictionary* goes on to suggest they are sufficiently described as "among the most lovable and influential of creations." While today we tend to think of poetic inspiration as less lovable than demonic, the description suggests that the terror from one's muse should arise from the terrible necessity of creation, rather than from fear by the woman poet that her social place may be denied and her social self assaulted. When women claim men's destiny and men's inspiration for their own, recognizing it as equally female with male, the question of muses will again become a literary nicety, the personification of art's infinite possibilities.

We have seen that contemporary women poets find it easier to express both their anger at the world and their imagination of female autonomy than do contemporary women novelists. Poetry, Adrienne Rich has told us, is "much more rooted in the unconscious, it presses too close against the barriers of repression." This explains, perhaps, why nineteenth century women, for the most part, wrote fiction and eschewed poetry. Even Elizabeth Barrett Browning, when she undertook to write of a woman's struggle toward selfhood, wrote a long narrative poem, *Aurora Leigh,* rather than lyrics. Charlotte and Emily Brontë, George Eliot, like Jane Austen, took up the novel as that form of expression, that construct, Rich says, which can be planned or organized to deal with one level at a time. "It is always what is under pressure in us, especially under pressure of concealment—that explodes in poetry."[51]

That women poets today can express what women novelists, for the most part, only discuss, consider, guess at, is, I think, a sign of great hope. If the woman's muse is such that it can inspire women poets, women novelists cannot be far behind. Women novelists so far have led their women heroes to the edge of selfhood: these heroes have managed, as we shall see, to desert marriage, but not to find another life. But the poets, particularly Adrienne Rich, have begun the task. In Rich's words: "No one has imagined us."

6

Marriage and Family

Marriage, in fiction even more than in life, has been the
woman's adventure, the object of her quest, her jour-
ney's end. Contemporary fiction modulates the formula
in one respect: the abandonment of marriage replaces
the achievement of it. While it is obvious what these
fictional women detest in marriage, it is not always clear
what they desire. How, indeed, might clarity be expected
about an institution defined to encompass, in women's
failure at autonomy, its own success?

So the women split: *Kinflicks, Small Changes, The*

Women's Room, Loose Ends, The Oracle—these are merely representative of a list too large for completion outside a funded study. What is new in these books is that we are seeing marriage at all—seeing it, moreover, from a woman's point of view. "What about Norm?" the narrator asks in *The Women's Room;* "Who is he, this shadow man, this figurehead husband?"[1] In fact, who Norm is, who all the husbands are, is clear: those who need someone to take care of their domestic, cooking, cleaning, sexual, breeding needs while they are out attending to civilization and their own appreciation of life. Even the least intelligent of husbands realize (and some of the most intelligent believe) that a change in marriage profound enough to satisfy the fleeing wives would profoundly alter that foundation of the conservative community, the family. Freud had urged women not to interfere with man in his pursuit of civilization, which is the way it is, the way men want it to be.

Earlier women writers put succinctly what they wanted: a chance to exercise their will, not vicariously but directly. Charlotte Brontë's Frances speaks in *The Professor:*

> Think of my marrying you to be kept by you, Monsieur! I could not do it; and how dull my days would be! . . . I like an active life better; I must act in some way, and act with you. I have taken notice, Monsieur, that people who are only in each other's company for amusement, never really like each other so well, or esteem each other so highly, as those who work together, and perhaps suffer together.[2]

Yet women writers for the most part, certainly in England, chose not to see the failure of marriage, if indeed they saw it at all, as something against which a woman might rise up. "Many who knew her," George Eliot writes of Dorothea Brooke, "thought it a pity that so substantive and rare a creature should have been absorbed into the life of another, and be known in a certain circle as a wife and mother. But no one stated exactly what else there was in her power she ought rather to have done." What else there is in a woman's power to do today is not much clearer, but at least she has one alternative not open to Dorothea: she can get out. And, in fiction and in life, she does.

How long it took the English novel to get around to examining marriage! English fiction down to the late nineteenth century dealt with the game of courtship endlessly, but with the business of marriage hardly at all. Where, as in Eliot, we see marriage, we observe, primarily, its failure. Thus in a world where courtship was the major action, we were shown few enough marriages to suggest the similarity, frequently noted, between marriage and war: both requiring, as Auden says, "patience, foresight, manoeuvre."

Married women in the English novel are, like Jewish women in Howe's *World of Our Fathers*, sustaining—think of Mrs. Bulstrode in *Middlemarch,* shut out from her husband's doings in the wide world, but ready to say to him, when the worst has happened, "Look up, Nicholas." If not prepared to be sustaining, women must be manipulative: like Rosamond in the same novel they use their feminine wiles to get what they want, which is not what their husbands want. If neither sustaining nor manipulative, they are simply happy in their wifely role, providing, like Mary Garth and her mother, the only sentimentalism in Eliot's powerful novel. As a good wife (the sort conservative thinkers regret in the confusion and complexity of the modern world), Mary Garth is pleased to have male children only. Who would wish for female children to repeat such a destiny, however "happily" undertaken? One of Doris Lessing's characters has observed: "Sometimes I dislike women, I dislike us all, because of our capacity for not-thinking when it suits us; we choose not to think when we are reaching out for happiness."[3] Who saw this better than George Eliot? Yet no solution presented itself to her fictive mind. Sustaining, manipulative, sentimental—or, like Dorothea, absorbed—there was no other imaginable possibility. Marriage remained, on the whole, unseen.

Jane Austen, Ronald Blythe tells us, "politely but firmly closes the bedroom doors . . . in our face. Courtship, like justice, has to be seen to be done, but the marriage ordeal is the most private thing in the world."[4] Austen's one happy couple, the Crofts in *Persuasion,* share his work in a constant companionship aboard ship, a pattern that, Wentworth tells the Crofts, he, the future Navy, will not allow. As for the other couples in Austen's novels, it is a nice but scarcely feverish debating point to decide which marriage is less satisfactory, the Bertrams in *Mansfield Park* or the Bennets in *Pride and Prejudice.* From the marriage of the Collinses in *Pride and Prejudice,* we prefer simply to avert our eyes.

Henry James and George Meredith began to look at marriage more steadily in the 1870s. The private ordeal of marriage began at that time to demand public scrutiny. The development was of course connected with the interest both novelists found in the female consciousness. To portray female destiny without examining marriage was like portraying male consciousness and not examining work and sex: impossible, unlikely, and dull.

Thus by the 1890s marriage, as Irving Howe observes in introducing *Jude the Obscure,* was becoming problematic.[5] Ibsen profoundly affected writers like Hardy. Sue Bridehead, in part responsible for her creator's abandonment of the novel form, managed to embody woman's confused response to matrimony and, in her final masochistic acceptance of it, to demonstrate why previous English novelists had preferred rather to defend the institution than to examine it.

"The abandonment of personality" is the prelude to love, Forster remarked in another novel about marriage in 1910. Making the same point, rather more delicately than Brontë but with no less acuity, he saw what woman in the contemporary novel was to discover as the price of wifehood: she must abandon herself. Indeed, if one imagined oneself as newly arrived from Mars and were to read the descriptions of a woman's marriage in contemporary novels by women, one might well ask how on earth anyone could be expected to live out such a farce. The answer of course is, as the man in Abraham Lincoln's story remarked while being carried out of town tarred and feathered on a rail, "for the honor of the thing." And the honor is as great as the shame of not marrying is horrific. Small wonder, then, that an opponent of the Equal Rights Amendment who fears vaguely for her marriage, should announce to a reporter: "I don't care to be a person."[6] She understood, while misunderstanding the ERA, that to be a person and a wife are oddly incompatible.

Why do contemporary men fail to see this? American male novelists have always been notoriously uninterested in female destiny; James, who got out of America and stayed out, is not so much an exception as an exile. By the 1960s, it seems, women were not even to be allowed the subject of domesticity any more, because they were using it not to exalt life indoors, but to dero-

gate it. James Dickey had this to say, for example, about
the poetry of Anne Sexton:

> It would be hard to find a writer who dwells more insistently
> on the pathetic and disgusting aspects of bodily experience,
> as though this made the writing more real, and it would also
> be difficult to find a more hopelessly mechanical approach to
> reporting these matters than the one she employs . . . her
> habitual gravitation to the domestic and the "anti-poetic"
> seems to me as contrived and mannered as any poet's harking
> after galleons and sunsets and forbidden pleasures.[7]

That Anne Sexton paid more attention to this review
than to all the good ones[8] is indicative of another female
characteristic that tends to bind the creature into marriage. But let us glance at a "domestic" poem from the
volume criticized:

Housewife

Some women marry houses.
It's another kind of skin; it has a heart,
 a mouth, a liver and bowel movements.
The walls are permanent and pink.
See how she sits on her knees all day,
 faithfully washing herself down.
Men enter by force, drawn back like Jonah
 into their fleshy mothers.
A woman *is* her mother.
That's the main thing.

In novel or poem, women have made it quite clear why
they are abandoning marriage. It is possible that Emily
Dickinson had said the same thing, though without the

"pathetic and disgusting aspects." Since she was never married, she might be supposed, when she wrote the following, not to be writing about marriage at all:

> To die—without the Dying
> And live—without the Life
> This is the hardest Miracle
> Propounded to Belief.

All men admire measured ways and wish women to embody them. Yeats's prayer for his daughter (like his annoyance at the Gore-Booth women for leaving Lissadell and riding off to combat), is wholly Yeats-oriented; he wants the still center of his spinning world to be a place of custom and ceremony, where innocence and beauty may be born. Let women take care of *that*. "Let her think opinions are accursed," Yeats wishes for his daughter, and live "rooted in one dear perpetual place." To Yeats, Con Markievicz became a bitter, abstract thing because she had not been content to remain clean and sweet, the beauty of her countryside.

So the historian Christopher Lasch scolds, echoing Yeats's tones. "The weakening of social ties . . . reflects a narcissistic defense against dependence."[9] It is clear to Lasch, as to other conservatives, that "the retreat to purely personal satisfactions" is disrupting the old ability to find roots in families, children, the future, and the past. He finds "one of the gravest indictments of our society is that it has made . . . lasting marriages so difficult to achieve." In growling about the search for personal fulfillment, Lasch does not particularly indict women, but neither does he seem to recognize that the old, good life, which he, Yeats, Trilling, and all today's new conservatives feel such nostalgia for, rested on the willingness of women to remain exactly where today's women, in fiction at least, will not remain: at home. Waiting for husband-warrior to retreat to them from the wide world is no longer enough.

Lasch is particularly harsh on what he sees as the cheap new ways to self-expression. Let Gail Sheehy try to identify the crises of life, and she will be dismissed by Lasch as a superficial assurer of "the anxious reader that conduct he finds puzzling or disturbing . . . can be seen as merely a normal phase of development."[10] Sheehy did not say that: what she did say is that the woman who finds herself miserable at home when she is supposed to have everything she has always wanted, everything all women have always wanted—this woman, who would, decades ago, have been sent home by her analyst in search of a vaginal orgasm—is now seen as passing through a stage of development recognized in men but not hitherto associated with women: adolescence. A woman is not an adolescent at puberty in our society, because her search for identity does not take place then:[11] rather it is a search for a husband in which she then engages. The search for self, Nora's search in Ibsen's *A Doll's House,* occurs deep into marriage and often with children left behind the slammed door. Sheehy's intention is not to placate, but to urge the recognition that dissatisfaction is human and risk is the price of life.

The real tension between Sheehy and Lasch, between the fleeing woman and those who struggle to preserve the family, is the tension between order and change, particularly evident in our society.[12] It is most evident within marriage, where the man desires order and the woman change. If the women are unclear about what change should encompass, they know it begins with their departure. Where they go when they leave the marriage has not yet been fully imagined, except for the two directions already traveled by women fleeing from the incarceration of wifehood: out, like Nora, or, like so many others, inward to the room of one's own.

Jane Wells, the wife of H.G. Wells, accepted the great scope of his life, his affairs, his adventures, but many years later took rooms in Bloomsbury, which Wells never saw. He wrote in his autobiography:

> She explained what she wanted and I fell in with her idea; and in this secret flat, quite away from all that life that centered upon me, she thought and dreamt and wrote and sought continually and fruitlessly for something she felt she had lost of herself or missed or never attained.[13]

In the Lower East Side ghetto in New York, Irving Howe tells us, young Jewish women recognized the same impulse. One wrote: "I wanted a room in which one simply sat. I had no clear idea of what I would do in it. But I had no room of my own. . . . Neighbors and relatives laughed in amusement at my wish."[14] The desire for what Woolf called a room of one's own became imperative: the only possibility for the achievement of a self, if not a self visible to the world, then at least a self discoverable deep, deep inside the house, or some house, where no one else could ever come.

Women forget that Woolf's advice to them was not only inward to a room of one's own, but outward also where their five-hundred pounds a year might be exchanged in a world of commerce. Woolf never advised withdrawal. In *Three Guineas* she admonished men that ruin could only follow "if you, in the immensity of your public abstractions forget the private figure, or if we in the intensity of our private emotions forget the public world."[15] The woman artist, like other artists, knew this instinctively: art is not often produced from a room sealed off from experience and interchange. Dickinson and Hopkins are dangerous models. So Woolf wrote Gerald Brenan: "I'm not sure that you shouldn't desert your mountain, take your chance, and adventure with your human faculties—friendships, conversations, relations, the mere daily intercourse."[16]

The current American women novelists take the message. Whatever their confusion or lack of specific purpose—their ambition, like Nora's, is great in its inexactitude—they at least know that if they first withdraw from their husband's presence, they do so to contemplate the possibility of wider adventures. To pick a novel almost at random, here is the heroine of Barbara Raskin's *Loose Ends,* secluded on a porch where she has spent nine hours a day writing a novel:

> Coco was outside on the second-floor back porch where she had spent every day since the first of June on the adjustable nylon lounge chair, which was now set at Semi-Recline and turned westward to catch the strong noonday sun. Everything that she needed was stationed around the long narrow porch. On the coffee table beside her was an ice bucket, two plastic tumblers, half a carton of Marlboro cigarettes, her electric portable typewriter, one oversize ashtray with a sandbag bottom, a Con-Tact-paper-covered English bisquit tin filled with beauty aids, three boxes of kitchen matches, a Snoopy alarm clock, Gavin's transistor radio, a can-opener, and one economy-size can of Raid repellent.[17]

On her porch, she is not only withdrawing dramatically from her family, she is planning her new life, and takes that first step in the reordering of one's energies: she makes a list.

1. Reorganize life
2. Write novel
3. Do women's-lib stuff for Housing Accomod. Commit.
4. Have Affair?
5. Find GOOD publisher
6. Take vacation alone
7. Take vacation with children to Yellowstone National Park?
8. Send children to Mother's!
9. Decide what to do in September
10. Get pregnant?
11. Fix house
12. Buy a farm
13. Get political—work for new Democratic nominee.[18]

Withdrawal toward an inner space of one's own begins, obviously enough, in an effort at simple self-preservation:

> I love to keep myself unto myself,
> To lock the door with exquisite finality

Elinor Wylie wrote.[19] One understands this exquisite finality the more readily in the light of a description of how a woman writer in the nineteenth century worked: "Her powers of concentration and her capacity for work were astounding . . . [Her son remembers that] 'everyone went into her library, we children, the servants, importunate visitors.' Always she was ready to drop her work when the children or her husband needed her."[20]

Small girls, at least those who grew up to become famous writers, have early in life begged for a room of their own and, we hear, got it. In 1846, Louisa May Alcott, who was then fourteen years old, wrote in her diary: "I have at last got the little room I have wanted so long, and am very happy with it. It does me good to be alone."[21] Willa Cather, at the same age, was given her own room in the attic, later described as Thea Kronberg's room in *The Song of the Lark:* "The acquisition of this room was the beginning of a new era in Thea's life. It was one of the most important things that ever happened to her. Hitherto, except in summer, when she could be out-of-doors, she had lived in constant turmoil. . . . The clamour about her drowned out the voice within herself."[22]

We do not read of boys begging rooms of their own. As a recent study of children's series books observed: "Boys act out their fantasies in the outside world, but girls retreat from their regular roles in the kitchen and parlor and contemplate their secret longings."[23] The boy's sense of self is formed outside, where the world is, not inside, where the safety is. Toni Morrison, speaking of her new novel, *Song of Solomon,* in an interview, said:

> I could not create the same kind of enclosed world that I had in previous books. Before it was as if I went into a room and shut the door in my books. I tried to pull the reader into that room. But I couldn't do that with Milkman [the hero of *Song of Solomon*]. It's a feminine concept—things happening in a room, a house. That's where we live, in houses. Men don't live in those houses, they really don't. My ex-husband is an architect and he didn't live there; every house is a hotel to him. So that the forces were different in this book, I had to look outward.[24]

Or, as a male biographer of a male subject put it, "He loved his home as a headquarters in which to rest between romantic sallies."[25]

In the nineteenth century novel, in England and America, there was no universe for women to move into, and even to seek out privacy within a novel like *Middlemarch* was to proclaim one's state of pain. Dorothea Brooke seeks solitude for reflection, but Mary Garth, the "happiest" woman in the novel, is never seen alone, but always in the midst of her family, children, men and women who have sought her out. In Eliot's earlier novel *The Mill on the Floss,* Maggie Tulliver seeks the ever-present female refuge, the attic, and at the end of the novel achieves the quintessential female privacy, death.

Death for women in literature is the ultimate room of one's own, and this has changed little, from Chopin's *The Awakening* just before the turn of this century, to a novel published recently. Perhaps the perfect expression of the woman's movement through selfhood to death is Doris Lessing's "To Room 19." This brilliant story tells of a young woman who has, as she says, "everything lonely women longed for." But what she has lost is herself, and she seeks a room "where no one would know where she was." In the end, she is found—her husband thinks she has a lover—in her shabby room in a run-down hotel, and on her last afternoon there she kills herself, because "without the room I don't exist."[26] For this woman, as for Edna in *The Awakening* and for many other women as well, death becomes the only part of their lives they can control. They can at least choose to die.

A recent English novel, *The Goat, the Wolf, and the Crab,* by Gillian Martin, recounts the last two years in the life of a housewife who is discovered to have operable cervical cancer. She refuses the operation, and the doctor considers her mad. She assures him that she is not in shock, and has made the decision. The doctor calls her insanely selfish. "Oh, yes," she answers. "Supremely selfish. It's the first autonomous decision of my life and the only one that is entirely selfish. I am thinking only of myself." She goes on:

> I am forty-two years old. My children are grown up. My husband is well employed. I have a marriage and a style of life that millions would envy. I have had my teeth looked at twice a year. I have had my eyes tested at suitable intervals, and, as you know, I have had cervical smears taken as recommended. I have done my washing on Mondays, cleaned out my cupboards regularly, and lain dutifully on my back and thought of England. I have kept my figure reasonably well and paid passing attention to changes in fashion. I have done everything as and when it was expected of me, and in the doing I have abdicated my self entirely. . . . In fact, I have not done anything at all without someone else's interests being the prime factor. This is the last opportunity. I insist on doing this in my own way.[27]

For many contemporary women novelists, however, the flight into life is now more interesting, if less easily charted, than the retreat into isolation, sanctuary, or death. Having moved from her refuge on the porch into the house, Raskin's heroine Coco is able to compose the following on her typewriter set up on the kitchen table:

> I would like to write a novel about an American woman who, after a lifetime of psychological dependency upon men —fathers, brothers, husbands, lovers, sons—self-consciously, but self-confidently, moves out front alone, on her own. I do not yet know the proper parable for this story, because I do not know yet what form such an experience takes. I do not know yet what scene will ensue, because it hasn't happened yet. But I would like to transcribe the metamorphosis of a female into a woman—of a woman into a human being—honestly, without cuteness, snideness, or self-

disparagement, and show how a woman learns to live without a man, just like a pioneer learns how to live in the wilderness —in order to survive.[28]

Woolf called her young male protagonist's place of being *Jacob's Room;* it is clear in the novel that Jacob's room has enlarged to become the universe: the wide world available to a young man of the upper classes in England before World War I. Jacob's life stood in contrast to that of the women he knew, to whom time was issued in "long white ribbons," which "they wind round and round and round and round."

Today women are also thinking of making their room the universe. What will happen to marriage if women do move out from the home, not into privacy alone but, as Woolf suggested, into the world? No one has yet imagined it in fiction, though more than a few today are living it.

"I have urged on Woman independence of Man," Margaret Fuller wrote almost a hundred and fifty years ago, "not that I do not think the sexes mutually needed by one another, but because in Woman this fact has led to an excessive devotion."[29]

The source of woman's "excessive devotion" is not far to seek: she fears that any assertiveness on her part will impair not only her femininity, which she might perhaps find the courage to risk, but the man's masculinity. Woman has convinced herself that man, in whom society and the family invest all power, is mysteriously fragile. He is fragile not before other men, who may fight with him in the street, tackle him on the playing field, contend with him in battle: he is frail before women, and offers as the price of woman's selfhood his own intact sexuality. Who can do justice to this riddle: man's superiority must not be challenged. It is a fact. At the same time, that superiority is so frail, that woman must contrive with man to sustain it.

Sylvia Plath, in 1957, wrote to her mother about the publication of her husband's first book of poems. "I am more happy than if it was my book published!" she wrote. "I have worked so closely on these poems of Ted's and typed them so many countless times through revision after revision that I feel ecstatic about it all." Sylvia Plath went on to become Sylvia Plath; we read her letters now, after her untimely death. But there are countless women who could have written that letter in the fifties, and none or few would have found its sentiments improper. She must assure her mother, since she is a poet (and many women who typed their husbands' poems and books, and sometimes researched and wrote them, had long since abandoned recognition of any accomplishment for themselves alone) that "I am so happy *his* book is accepted *first*. It will make it so much easier for me when mine is accepted. . . ." Plath's mother adds a footnote to this letter assuring us that from the time she was a very little girl, Sylvia "catered to the male of any age so as to bolster his sense of superiority." In seventh grade she was glad to come in second in a spelling contest. It is nicer, she felt, to have a boy *first.* [30]

Little more than twenty years later, we read this account with some amazement. The degree to which women had internalized their own punishment if they should succeed beyond their husband, or any male, is difficult to describe today in all its intensity.

Hanna Papenek reports, however, that such fears were, until very recently, common. "Openly acknowledged collaboration in the context of a two-person career, is not very frequent. The ambivalence surrounding the wife's contribution suggests that many institutions, again particularly in the academic world, recognize the fragility of male self-esteem in American society, and have adopted a number of ways of safeguarding it."[31] Among western nations, few display more rigid sexual stereotyping than America. All overt power is given to the male. In this society the possibility of men's failure is interpreted to mean not that power should be shared, but that the fear of losing it should be indulged.

Sexually, women fear male impotence, fear any blow to the male sexual ego. At the same time that the male is raping and foraging on the streets, his counterpart, in bed with the woman or in dialogue with the woman, is seen in constant danger of intimidation. The penis may collapse, crushing the male ego and the marriage in its flaccidity. It is hard to know how we arrived there, unless one realizes that to worship the totem of superiority is to protect it: it is the key to success for both partners in a marriage, not only literally, but figuratively.

I have discussed this matter with a woman friend of mine, a writer but no feminist, with no real interest in women, but of high and rigorous intelligence. She defends the fragility of men, with whom she identifies far more readily than with women. First of all, their exposed sexual organ is in constant danger of mutilation. It is exposed, it can be struck. Freud is her first and most vigorous ally here. She will not recognize that this metaphor for weakness is granted to those with absolute cultural strength and power, so that they may have an excuse to exercise their power.

Fragility of men is her experience, she tells me simply. Her father, her uncles, all the men in her family, in her experience, have been fragile beside the strong women who dominated them. They became fragile because they were not encouraged in manliness, because their wives and mothers, with no expression of energy open to them save vicarious accomplishment, drove them too hard, at home and at work. If a farmer drives his horse too hard, we may think it unkind or unwise, but it does not occur to us to grant the horse unusual fragility.

Dora Ullian has studied the attitudes of girls toward society's demand that they be supportive of men. From six to ten in the stage Ullian calls Assertion, she found that girls resent boys. From ten to fourteen, they begin to swerve toward support of them, the stage Ullian calls Ambivalence. By fourteen, girls have accepted the need of underpinning males and have entered the stage she calls Accommodation. Ullian has many explanations, ranging from the tininess of boys and their penises to the training of girls in supportive behavior, all of which are valid. Boys are less like the men they aspire to be than girls are like women.[32] Probably far more essential, however, is the woman's need, in her hunger for dependency and her fear of autonomy, to find a self-sacrificing reason for her secondary role.

As I write this, the wonderful face of Tillie Olsen appears before my eyes; I remember her in my office at the Radcliffe Institute, full of earnestness, persuading me not to blame women. How blame them when even the most fortunate of them has never had a chance? Do I not know what the life of women is? Any woman who writes, even for a short time, Tillie proclaims, is a survivor.

It is not, I try to assure her (unsuccessfully, I know), a matter of blame. I want to name what it is that holds women in thrall. I have worked with enough males, heard them joking cruelly about women, not to underestimate the power of men to oppress. But I wish to shock women, if need be, into the realization that one sex cannot be burdened with the psychic survival of the other, that such an arrangement is not ordained.

We are all of us, men and women, complex, superior one moment, frail and helpless the next. We need support, comfort, ego-satisfaction, love. We are wicked when we achieve that satisfaction only in self-denial—I use the word wicked in the sense Jesus meant when speaking of buried talents. We turn to one another in our pain in every relationship known. We strive for companionship in which there is no one absolutely dependent, no one absolutely superior. We find the inability of a man to have sex terrifying—a man paralyzed in a car accident has written an entire book about the efforts of various women and himself to allow him sexuality[33]—yet the readiness of societies and cultures, let alone individual men, to allow women sexuality, let alone strive for it, is only recently recorded.[34]

Marriage is now failing before our eyes, but its preservation depends upon the restructuring of the family, where "strength" and "weakness," "fragility," and "endurance" are not assigned by gender. The irony here, as in all essentially reactionary positions, is that those most interested in preserving the family in its nineteenth century form are, in that very act, destroying its cornerstone, marriage. For, as Nancy Chodorow has brilliantly demonstrated, our present family structure produces children incapable of the very heterosexual love it has tried to inculcate. In insisting upon "mothering" as the function only of one female figure, we have made impossible the companionship of men and women.

Marriage can be preserved only if we allow family structure to change. Institutions that cannot adapt will not survive. That is the lesson conservatives stubbornly refuse to learn, perhaps because admitting its truth fatally weakens the logic of their position.

Oddly enough, one of the most revolutionary voices in American fiction about family roles and the expectations of girls in confronting them is to be found in one of the standard works of children's fiction. Early in *Little Women* Jo March tells us: "I hate affected, nimin-piminy chits. . . . I hate to think I've got to grow up and be Miss March, and wear long gowns and look as prim as a China-aster. . . . I can't get over my disappointment in not being a boy." Jo is assured by Beth that she is a brother to them all; in her father's absence, she declares herself to be "the man of the family."

Jo plays the male parts in plays, she wears a "gentlemanly" collar and has a gentlemanly manner, she thinks of herself as a businessman and cherishes a pet rat. (The pet rat is male and has a son, "proud of his whiskers," who accompanies him along the rafters.) Jo finds it easier to risk her life for a person than to be pleasant when she doesn't want to, and she admires the "manly" way of shaking hands. The point is clear enough: men's manners speak of freedom, openness, camaraderie, physical abandon, the chance to escape passivity. Who would not prefer such a destiny, except those taught to be afraid?

A woman writer has here imagined, as she has lived, the truths of revolutionary girlhood. But as with so many women writers, Alcott could not sustain it.[35] She marries off Jo and allows her to devote herself to a school for boys (who would want to bother with girls?) and presents, in Meg's children, as perfect a description of stereotypical upbringing within a nuclear family as has ever been afforded us:

At three, Daisy demanded a "needler," and actually made a bag with four stitches in it; she likewise set up housekeeping in the sideboard, and managed a microscopic cooking-stove with a skill that brought tears of pride to Hannah's eyes, while Demi learned his letters with his grandfather. . . . The boy early developed a mechanical genius. . . . Of course, Demi tyranized over Daisy, and gallantly defended her from every other aggressor; while Daisy made a galley-slave of herself, and adored her brother as the one perfect being in the world.

Etcetera, unfortunately. Perhaps only in America, with its worship of "manliness," could boy-girl twins, elsewhere universally a literary phenomenon characterized by their resemblance to one another, be so sharply defined and differentiated by sex roles. It is no wonder that Alcott never married; an all-girl family had not prepared her for service to the family's son: she *was* the family's "son."

In reexamining marriage and the family, we might begin with the observation of fact, looking at modern marriage directly, recording what is happening to it in the world around us. Or we might start by examining theory, looking at the revisions that Chodorow and others have proposed in the interpretation of the Oedipus complex, that classic theoretical construct that relates personality development to family structure. Either way, we are led inexorably to the conclusion that marriage and parenting must change if marriage and the family are to be saved as viable institutions.

Freud's characterization of the processes of infancy is based on the definition of gender as the presence or absence of masculinity.[36] Boys are defined as having a penis, girls as being deprived of it. (Freud called them,

simply, "castrated.")[37] All the destiny boys and girls encounter arises from this difference. In fact, as Chodorow
has brilliantly demonstrated, these anatomical differences are not essential to Freud's account of the Oedipus
complex; it is possible to reconstruct his account so that
it encompasses the experience of all children, whether
boys or girls.

But we must realize that parenting as it has formerly
been practiced (where only the mother, or a single female substitute, can properly care for the infant) re-
produces the very sexual bias in the children that origi-
nally inspired Freud to *his* sexual bias. If you bring
children up with a mother in constant attendance, as the
only object of early infant bonding, and if the father is
largely absent and comes to represent to the growing
infant the only alternative to the mother's encompassing
love, you will precisely reproduce the family condition
that will impel girls toward mothering and boys to seek
their destiny in the world apart from parenting. They in
turn will establish that marriage, that family, which statis-
tical observation confirms as unviable.

What is the solution? How can we change the conditions we have today? On the one hand, boys, nurtured
only by a woman, seek separation from her as the price
of their maleness. On the other hand, girls, because they
do not fully separate from the mother, experience themselves as less differentiated than boys as individuals,[38]
while remaining more in touch with the inner world they
shared with their same-sex mother. For girls, the first
intimacy with the mother remains, and for that reason
they find it easier to love and to be intimate. They may
become "genitally heterosexual," but the object of their
love will always be, to some extent, women, and they
must be bound to their husbands, and isolated from

other women, by family strictures whose main purpose is to increase their dependency upon their husband. At the same time, boys, in a nuclear family, develop more "rigid ego boundaries" than girls and a more distinct sense of themselves as selves; but their masculine personality comes to be defined as the denial of relation.[39]

What becomes clear is that this family structure, designed to produce the gender stereotyping we have so long experienced, denies to men and women any real sense of each other as the object of profound intimacy. Men define themselves by their separation from women; women define themselves by their lack of separation, of selfhood. In the absence of those special factors that produce achieving women, they will cling to the male as husband and, in that role, as the definer of their identity.

There is only one solution to this problem: a family structure in which both parents care for the children in equal turns, and where parental substitutes (who should themselves be few and constant) are of both sexes. Neither boys nor girls will then identify separation as separation from the mother, nor conceive of the only alternative to her and her all-encompassing love as inevitably male.

There is a pattern for such marriage: what the Rapoports have called the Dual-Career Family.[40] It is perhaps well to remember at this point that what has so far been conventionally practiced is the Two-Person Career, where the man has the career, and the woman sustains him in it. As the divorce rate and other factors indicate, this has not been a successful pattern, to say the least. The latest example of its growing weakness is the increasingly frequent refusal of men to move from one location to another at the behest of national companies: they decline more and more to dislocate their wives in this formerly acceptable way.

The Dual-Career Family was first described by the Rapoports in the 1960s, when the term was new and the concept considered eccentric. The revised edition of their book indicates that the concept is now widely discussed and the term found in general use. The Rapoports describe the Dual-Career Family as that "type of family structure in which both heads of household—the husband and the wife—pursue active careers and family lives." The Rapoports define "career" as "those types of job sequences that require a high degree of commitment and that have a continuous developmental character."[41] Such a family structure not only allows the woman freedom to develop an identity not defined by her relationship to a man, but also rescues the man from the assumption that, for all practical purposes, he does not have a family at all, only a profession or job.

The Rapoports describe how the "myth of motherhood"[42] served, when their original study was published, as a major argument against the Dual-Career Family. However, their examples of Dual-Career families indicate, as does the experience of many of those who have taken part in or closely observed these dual-career arrangements, that in fact the children are enriched rather than deprived by the double parenting. The "myth of motherhood" has lost some of its power recently, but what has arisen in its place is the fear that, if the individual mother does not remain sole caretaker, the child will be abandoned to no care at all.

The birth of a child must come to be seen universally as a profound event: not the distant result, often accidental, of sexuality. We shall probably come to recognize before too long the essential rightness of those earlier peoples who denied or ignored the relation between sex and childbirth. That children should arrive in the world, unwelcome and unprepared for, as the consequence of lust or sexual pleasure, is no longer supportable as an ideal except by the most retrograde theories of human behavior.

Childbirth must be seen as the commitment of two people, especially because of past history, as the commitment of the *father*, who must devote himself equally with the mother to the infant he calls into being. From such a commitment will arise not only the benefits of the symmetrical family, but the initiation of men into intimacy and nurturance of which they have been long deprived, and which follows from the care of wanted children. From birth onward, the child must be held in its father's arms no less than in its mother's, and experience male love.

Some years ago friends of ours adopted an infant. It seemed to me then that the whole process of their commitment—to the child, to their continuing individual careers—celebrated his arrival in ways often lost to the child naturally born to an unprepared couple. It happened that this child was adopted from abroad and the involvement of two governments in his arrival seemed properly to mark the importance of such an event. What has only occurred to me now is that this child's arrival, and his parents' loving commitment to him for the next fifteen years, had nothing to do with sexuality, a part of their marriage not intrinsically connected with the arrival of a child: the wisdom of so-called primitives is often profound.

Furthermore, sexuality itself, we now know, has suffered in the last two centuries from its vision of itself as a mechanism for reproduction. Nonsense, such as the wholly vaginal orgasm and the primacy of male orgasm, arises from just such a mechanistic view. The sexuality of which men and women are capable is only now beginning to be recognized as comprising more than that rapid, largely impersonal act necessary to reproduction.

Women must retain control of their own bodies, including the decision of whether or not to carry a child within them. At the same time, men must acquire control of their fatherhood—and choose acts of procreation only when they intend to endow the resulting child with time and attention. We may then begin to mystify fatherhood not, as in the past, as some distant, godlike, authority figure, but as a parent, like the mother, partaking of daily adventures in intimacy and affection.

Indeed, the "symmetrical family," as it can also be called, has, in the 1970s, been recognized as the emergent family form, still in the minority but "destined to be the dominant family form in the future."[43] It should by now be clear that the old style family structure is not only crumbling, but where it persists, it is, in fact, making *more* likely the very conditions that the defenders of conventional family life most deplore: homosexuality, divorce, and casual sex. I am not certain that heterosexual love and marriage are as vital as Anita Bryant and her supporters think they are; what I do know is that the "normalcy" she so vigorously champions is best produced by marriages that share more with friendship than with romance, and by families where the care of the children from birth on is divided between individuals of both sexes.

The sexual divison of labor, Chodorow tells us, produces male dominance. And male dominance produces men incapable of loving, and women incapable of selfhood. From this division we must turn. As Martin Buber has written:

The sins which man commits—these are not his high crime. Temptation is powerful and his strength is slight! The great crime of man is that he can turn at every moment, and does not do so![44]

And the Bible supports him in this. For it is written:

On the one hand, a former commandment is set aside because of its weakness and uselessness (for the law made nothing perfect); on the other hand, a better hope is introduced.[45]

I think that the goals of women's societies should be to self-destruct. The most talented women should not be in women's groups but in men's groups. That's where the power is.

ROSALYN YALOW, Nobel prizewinner for medicine[1]

> *I have to cast my lot with those*
> *who age after age, perversely,*
> *with no extraordinary power,*
> *reconstitute the world.*

ADRIENNE RICH, "Natural Resources" [2]

The Claims of Woman

There appeared in 1977 a volume of essays in honor of Lionel Trilling. Conceived as a Festschrift, it became per force a memorial volume. Two essays struck me as stating between them the situation of marriage, parenthood, women, and the search for the self as they were, so to speak, at Trilling's death, as they will, without the determined efforts of a sufficient number of women, remain through another period of retreat from feminism.

Robert Adams, in an essay entitled "Religion of Man, Religion of Woman,"[3] discusses the development of man's quasi-religious veneration of woman in the nineteenth century. In 1860 Michelet celebrated woman as simultaneously (or perhaps sequentially?) the creator of babies and the recreator of her husband, who regenerates him "by perpetual acts of trust and submission." Michelet assumes, Adams points out, that "the bourgeois family is the ultimate and definitive form of social organization, with the wife as both tyrant and prisoner of that snug unit." By the late nineteenth century worshippers at the shrine of womanhood placed her "outside the world of culture. . . . As the stream through which nature flows—universal, instinctive, always seeking its own level—woman is both sacred and obscene, sacred as redeeming man from culture, obscene as content with a merely appetitive existence. . . ." The literary elaboration of the religion of woman culminated in Joyce's *Finnegan's Wake,* when woman became "nothing but a flowing and a circulation," redeeming the world by "throwing away the quarrelsome logic and endless guilt of the masculine mind. . . ." Adams ends with a suggestion that time may render this formulation obsolete.

No other essay in the Trilling Festschrift takes up the question of women, either in life or in literature: she remains outside the culture, indeed! Daniel Bell's paper, however, is significant for the context in which it ignores the question.

"Beyond Modernism, Beyond Self" suggests, in keeping with Trilling's ideas, that we must move past the narcissistic and egocentric concern with self to the thought of the community, if we are not to disrupt the coherence of life "in the name of an unbounded self." In the nineteenth century, Bell reminds us:

The sense of the self comes to the fore. The individual comes to be considered as individual, with singular aspirations, and life assumes a greater sanctity and preciousness. The enchantment of the single life, its pain and fear assuaged, becomes a value for its own sake. Economic meliorism, antislavery sentiment, women's rights, the end of child labor and cruel punishment, education for all, were the social issues of the day. But in the deeper metaphysical sense the idea of progress and the vision of material plenty became the basis for the idea that men could go beyond necessity, that they would no longer be constrained by nature but could arrive—in Hegel's phrase—at the end of history.[4]

Professor Bell's disapproval of all this fairly crackles from the page. For our purposes, he but echoes Trilling. Women's rights he recognizes only as a social issue in the nineteenth century. In making his case against the disruptive consequences of man's achievement of an unbounded self, he does not notice that "man" is male, and that woman may have yet a few bounds to overreach before achieving the selfhood that man has gloried in for one hundred fifty years. For man, pushing beyond nature meant overcoming the constraint of poverty, a feat now largely accomplished in the West. For woman it meant, in addition, first overcoming the bondage of endless childbearing and, next, destroying the imprisoning myth of motherhood, tasks only half-accomplished in the West, even now. It is woman's misfortune still to be seeking individual fulfillment at a moment in history when what Professor Bell conceives to be man's excesses are already giving selfhood a bad name.

Men today in Bell's world, visible to him, do not need to construct a self: every aspect in their lives has conspired to construct it for them, to encourage them in the enjoyment of it. Women, meanwhile, have played for men the roles of nurturer and partaker of meekness: they have been willing, not to inherit the earth, but to wait patiently to inherit it from those who will honor their achieved meekness.

It takes, obviously, a Daniel Bell or a Lionel Trilling to say to the world: selfhood is to be denigrated, is to be seen as selfish, sinful, and denying society of its just coherence. One is reminded of the Victorian patriarch telling an impoverished child to bear with fortitude the destiny to which God has called her.

Many, while understanding this, will ask if, all the same, selfhood is what women should aspire to. Would it not be better to shatter the "sorry scheme of things entire" and build a different society in which the ends of the individual and the claims of community might merge so harmoniously that the individual would not feel compelled by social power, nor the community threatened by the imperial self? Men and women together may aspire to that end and may even achieve it within small communities of the likeminded. For the larger society, however, it seems to me too remote a possibility to divert our attention from the here and now in which women must live or lose their lives. I am convinced, therefore, that we must continue the struggle for female selfhood, unfortunately now rendered even more arduous by a rising conservative opposition, which from its bastions of power exalts the claims of a community still devoted to the protection of male privilege.

I wish to speak a bit about power, and my experience of it—not of having it, which I have not done, but of having observed it closely in the last several years. Only the woman's movement has brought me close enough to power to observe it.

Power believes it has the truth and the ability to implement it. Above all, it refuses to look at any truth that has so far evaded it. So Trilling would not look at women and their particular problems—his truth did not encompass that. When a woman finds a "truth," as did, for example, Mary Baker Eddy, the hardening of the truth into institution and empire is taken over by men. Those women who oppose the takeover are exiled and forgotten. Wellesley's President has recently defended volunteerism—the career of most of the college's contributors and rich alumnae—because of all the social innovations volunteers were responsible for: child labor laws, religious and infant schools, even perhaps abolition.[5] What Wellesley's President did not mention is that, once underway, each of these reforms was taken over by men: power moved in. Women have been unable either to establish power or to invade it. At Columbia, I have heard men say, with perfect sincerity, that a few women seeking equal pay are trying to overturn the university, to ruin it. High administrators may be forced to respond to some government pressure, but the idea that their university might be in any way improved by the fuller admission of women into its ranks strikes them as simply ludicrous.

In my observation of power in recent years, I have learned that however hard women try to win the admiration and support of male power, they never succeed. They are like lower class men admitted into elite clubs: they are never certain that one must not be to the manner born, and they are right. After itself, power most respects countervailing power. Having long been among women who were careful never to offend the males in power, several of us have discovered that in fighting power we achieved more in a month than submission had accomplished in years. That is why those who speak of slow change for women speak with no knowledge of power. Power is like an amoeba. Sufficiently jolted by an external particle, it will eventually absorb it and make it part of itself, changing, of course, in the process. Power is self-satisfied. Token women, and those men power uses but does not respect, are the tools of power. The women or men who fight power are the only ones with effect. Perhaps that is what Rich meant about the power of the powerless. The token woman, though she may have the delusion of power, is without effect upon the world, less consequential than the merest housewife. She works through men, and offers nothing of service to other women. On the scale of power, she is a second-rate man, even if her mind is twice that of her colleagues'.

Looking back, for a moment, to the quotations which head this chapter, one sees the two choices women have been encouraged to make in regard to men and power: join them, or undermine them, become an honorary man, or a counter-cultural force. My own experience, growing up in a postwar, strongly patriarchal society and working within a major university, is that neither way will suffice. Women must want to be where the power is, but they must want to be there as women, and in large numbers.

I think women should be urged to enter the world of power, but they ought not to fool themselves about the personal cost: it is great. At the same time I would, from my own experience, urge on women the faith that a moment does come when the cruelty and anger of the men in power, if it does not cease, at least ceases to wound.

Women have, I think—and I with them for at least half my professional life—recoiled before the first experience of male attack upon their femininity. It is a moment that

I surmise is close to the experience of rape: men's aim is to tell women that her sole destiny is for male uses. Men who would not dream of sneering at Blacks, or Jews (and certainly those who would), can be confident of hearty male support (and some female support, too) if they make jokes about women. And because women have so long been told that to be shrill, or emotional, or argumentative is reprehensible in the circles of power, the merest hint that they are transgressing is enough to silence most of them. But, we must ask ourselves, who made the rules? This is indeed a nice question, since almost every achieving woman has told us she has managed not to offend men, and has yet succeeded. What then, she asks, is all the fuss about?

Recently, I was asked to read a manuscript for a major university press. The woman editor who called me said, with an edge of anger in her voice: "The manuscript is *not* one of those strident feminist theses." Indeed, this editor, who signed herself "Mrs. John Jones" in correspondence, sounded far more strident and self-righteous than any feminist I had heard in years. Thus does the male club dehumanize those it accepts. Such women, however, grow older and fewer in number.

If the cost of fighting power is great, so are the rewards. We have heard little of this. Here again, I can speak best of my own experience, and that of one of my University colleagues. When it became clear that we indeed intended to speak out, not only for women, but for the standards of performance and attention to students we considered important, the force of the personal attacks we sustained at first almost crushed us. The disapproval and disdain were palpable, a dense Dickensian fog. Everything we said was dismissed as "hysterical." The males in power became unable to hear us; they heard only what they expected to hear. They did not hesitate to pass comment behind our backs on everything from our sanity to our sexual "normality." They adamantly resisted granting us equal pay for equal accomplishment.

I mention this because I do not want to minimize the hardship women bear in fighting for their beliefs within male institutions; hardship, it should be added, that we felt despite our positions of great strength: we had tenure, full personal lives, strong academic reputations, and each other. We noticed, furthermore, that men who were at each other's throats on every other issue could be brought to unite against the demands of women with a well-aimed joke and a knowing chuckle. If we, who had so much going for us, felt threatened and disillusioned and afraid, what might other women feel who did not have our advantages?

The answer, I think, is very like the conclusion of the *Wizard of Oz,* or the story of the Emperor's New Clothes, like many of those stories women have not thought to apply to the female condition. Suddenly, one sees the men in power clearly. The whole paraphenalia of stardom that had clung to them falls away. They lose their trappings of high office, and become no more than frightened individuals (perhaps just a little nastier and sillier than other people). But don't they still have the power? Yes. But so do you. Once the pyrotechnic of power ceases to dazzle, and power becomes mere sticks and powder and hoopla, a kind of energy returns to frightened women. Their own fear is what women have most to overcome—their fear, and their anxiety about being aggressive, nonconciliatory. Once that fear and anxiety lessen, the ways to power become more evident, more usable.

In my own experience, moreover, I have found that if one acts with courage, one finds unexpected, unaccustomed allies. Men here and there, younger men, and some older men of extraordinary quality, offer support. So do many younger women. I am often asked by younger feminist women who do not have permanent faculty appointments if they ought to fight the power structure before gaining tenure. It is not a question I can answer. How can one urge upon others courage that is not required of oneself? But younger women can at the least offer quiet support to the older women who stand and fight.

I have been amazed at the fear of male disapproval often expressed by women with tenure. Some years ago Columbia women joined in a class action suit to test in the courts their right to equal pension payments with men. In fact, the Supreme Court has since, in a similar case, found for the women, and there was never much question in the mind of anyone who had looked into it that such would be the outcome. Yet only fourteen of all the tenured women faculty in Columbia University signed the class action complaint (only five of the fourteen tenured women from 1971) while almost one hundred untenured women, mainly untenured administrators, signed it. We must build on the hope that these facts encourage, that female fear is lessening.

For as I look now at that list of names, I know that I hold in my hand the evidence of woman's servitude and dependency. Woman has not, like Demeter, used what she had to force her rights upon men. Rather, she has willingly relinquished her rights and those of younger women, accepting in their place the role of "other" of, as Simone de Beauvoir told us so long ago, the "Second Sex." At the time of our class action suit, one of the tenured women wrote a letter explaining why she would not sign. If women make trouble, she asked, surely the University will not continue to hire them. When it was pointed out to her that the University had not hired many women, despite their years of quiet acquiescence, she answered, inevitably, *I* made it.

Those in power, like those in Dante's Hell, go on doing what they are doing. Without pressures from outside, they never change. Resistance to genuine dialogue is one of the chief signs of power. Women must continue to invade the domains of power in order to change institutions as we know them, in order to offer places to other women, in order to offer all children the possibility of testing their abilities, and, finally, in order to do justice to themselves.

Louise Bogan wrote in her journal that, toward her mother, her "earliest instinct was to protect—to take care of, to endure." This, her analyst once told her, "is the instinct of a little boy." Well, Bogan adds, "there it is. I *did* manage to become a woman."[6]

And then there are Virginia Woolf's words. "One makes up the better part of life." But women have made up so little. They have been told that all their instincts to fabrication, to protection are male. Today, the question of whether the human condition is indeed differentiated between the male and the female, and must remain irremediably so, is of profound importance, and not alone to conservatives. Feminists, too, are divided. Two interpretations of history, which we may, for convenience, call the French and the American, today declare male and female to be eternally and irreversibly differentiated.

French feminists believe that a permanent distinction

between the sexes is imbedded in language. Following the theoretical work of Lacan and Derrida, they analyze language, finding it, throughout history, both phallocentric and "written out": that is, male history is the text we know, and is exhausted. The psychic structuring of women cannot, in their opinion, be changed, but it can be written into a language so as to express the female through a new language, female-centered. Though I speak hesitantly in this area, it does seem to me that this theory implies a belief in the separation of women from the patriarchal culture, the better to develop the female language.

American interpretations of the fundamental diversity of the sexes, following the methods of the social sciences, are more empirical, less theoretical. According to this argument, women are sharply distinguished from men by hormonal and genetic codings that render inevitable the female care of infants and the female nurturing disposition. In no way, these Americans assure us, can such codings be reversed.[7]

These convictions of the irreversible distinction between the sexes must, I think, be disregarded if we are serious about reinventing womanhood. Certainly, there can be no question of the historical distinctions between the sexes: women have been participants in culture, but without history; their collective memory has been buried in darkness and must be brought up from that darkness. History is a male account. Yet I question whether the past divisiveness is incumbent upon the future.

The American interpretation I consider both wholly mistaken and profoundly dangerous for women. The biological "facts" on which these convictions of sexual determination are based are thought by many prominent biologists to be insubstantial. In addition, the American interpretation seems to me to be the outgrowth of fear, and to follow the old pattern of female retreat into patriarchally condoned "mainstream" interpretations. The French theories, on the other hand, strike me as full of possibility and high intelligence. Though I do not myself believe that this separate, collective reconstruction of language and culture will eventuate in great advance for women, I recognize it as a brave undertaking whose outcome cannot yet be foreseen. Womanhood must be reinvented by those who can imagine, not by those who wish to reconstruct their gender prison.

So far, it is men who have moved upon the earth and had adventures; it is men who have told stories. But—and this has been too little noticed—the men have told stories about women as well as about men. The nearer one comes to an oral tradition, the more noticeable this becomes. The Murphys, as anthropologists, for example, tell us that among the forest people, the men have many stories about women, but the women have none about men.[8]

The Murphys suppose that men fear women, as women do not fear men—deep, that is, in the subconscious where reassurance is most essential. Certainly men, who have had only female parenting, think back with fear, desire, and horror to the best, lost love. Certainly they resent its departure and search, unsuccessfully, for its replacement.

But perhaps women have not told stories because there were no stories to tell. There was only the dailiness of life, the attention to food, clothing, shelter, the endless replication of motherhood. At the end of *Little Women,* Demi learns the alphabet; he invents; he protects; he discovers. Daisy only sews what has been torn, cooks what will be eaten, and asks for love. In what story could Daisy think of herself as the protagonist, except in the story of the man who will come to give her the home where her cooking and sewing will be done?

A few years ago, my daughter Margaret spent the summer in London working as a volunteer for the Royal Anthropological Institute. Thinking it would interest me, she brought back this account of an Albanian tribe, the Klementi, described by a woman explorer early in the twentieth century:

> All marriages were arranged by the heads of the families and the younger people had no say in the matter; the daughters of a family or tribe were chattels to be disposed of as best to advantage the family; if girls objected fiercely to being sent away to an unknown man, much cruelty and force was sometimes used to breach the girl's will; the bridegroom's family was deeply insulted and a blood feud might arise; this could only be avoided by the girl swearing an oath before twelve witnesses that she would never marry; she then ranked as a man, might, and often did, wear men's attire, eat with the men (which no other women did), smoke with them and carry weapons; such women were known as "Albanian virgins" and worked as herdsmen of sheep and goats. . . .[9]

It occurred to me that the women of that tribe, like the unusual women in our culture, knew that the way to escape bondage was to be accepted as a man: it was as simple as that. Not easy, but simple. Clear. Their numbers, however, were few, and the price of the transformation was high, nothing less than their womanhood.

These Klementi virgins, the women at Columbia in 1971, Hennig's women, all insisted that they too could learn, invent, discover. They paid for their accomplishments by giving up their identity with other women, their pride in the women of their society, their culture, their civilization, their ability to imagine other women like themselves. They became honorary men and joined the all-male club, whether in herding sheep and goats, teaching in a university, or working in the business world.

But there is another way, the choice of Jo: to appropriate the male model without giving up the female person. The young woman must learn, as Jo did, to tell herself stories and to act in plays, in which she, a female, is the protagonist. Jo reinvented girlhood, but the task of reinventing womanhood was beyond her. Even so, while telling herself stories in which she was the protagonist, she remained in a community of women;[10] she did not desert or demean them, or look upon them as less worthy than herself.

The past is male. But it is all the past we have. We must use it, in order that the future will speak of womanhood, a condition full of risk, and variety, and discovery: in short, human.

Notes

Notes to Chapter 1—

Personal and Prefatory (pp. *15* to *36*)

1. Charlotte Perkins Gilman, *The Living of Charlotte Perkins Gilman* (New York: Harper & Row, 1975), p. 74.

2. For someone who agrees, see Nora Ephron, "Reunion," in *Crazy Salad* (New York: Alfred A. Knopf, 1975), pp. 28–36.

3. Samuel Ornitz, *Haunch, Paunch and Jowl;* quoted in Jay Martin, *Nathanael West* (New York: Farrar, Straus & Giroux, 1970), p. 13.

4. Mimi Kelber, "The UN's Dirty Little Secret," *Ms.*, November 1977, p. 80.

5. *Boston Globe*, 9 January 1977.

6. *New York Times*, 7 January 1977. I am grateful to Grace Baruch for drawing my attention to this item.

7. *New York Times Book Review*, 9 October 1977.

8. Nancy Chodorow, *The Reproduction of Mothering: Psychoanalysis and the Sociology of Gender* (Berkeley: University of California Press, 1978), p. 40. Later discussions will make clear my great reliance on this important book.

9. Alexis de Tocqueville, *Recollections*, trans. A. T. de Mattos (New York: Macmillan, 1896), p. 101.

10. Chodorow, *The Reproduction of Mothering*, p. 9.

Notes to Chapter 2—

Woman as Outsider (pp. 37 to 70)

1. Lionel Tiger, *Men in Groups* (New York: Vintage Books, 1970), p. 40. It is, perhaps, unnecessary for me to add that Tiger's book is particularly valuable as an example of the ardent masculinist point of view.

2. Carroll Smith-Rosenberg, "The Female World of Love and Ritual: Relations between Women in Nineteenth-Century America," *Signs* (Autumn 1975), pp. 1–30.

3. See, in this connection, Nancy F. Cott, *The Bonds of Womanhood* (New Haven: Yale University Press, 1977).

4. Virginia Woolf, *Three Guineas* (New York: Harcourt, Brace & Company, 1938), pp. 162, 166.

5. Robert Fitzgerald, "Postscript," to *The Odyssey*, trans. Robert Fitzgerald (Garden City: Anchor Books, 1963), p. 506.

6. Ann Ulanov in *The Feminine*, quoted in Caroline Whitbeck, "Theories of Sex Difference," in *Women and Philosophy*, ed. Carol G. Gould

and Marx W. Wartofsky (New York: Capricorn Books, 1976), p. 66. Emphasis added.

7. Ray Strachey, *The Cause: A Short History of the Women's Movement in Great Britain* (1928; reprinted. Port Washington, N.Y.: Kennikat Press, 1969), p. 75.

8. *Ibid.*, p. 285.

9. Cecil Woodham-Smith, *Florence Nightingale* (New York: Grosset & Dunlap, 1951), p. 259.

10. Adrienne Rich, *Of Woman Born* (New York: W.W. Norton, 1976), p. 193.

11. *Ibid.*, p. 195.

12. *Ibid.*, p. 285.

13. The term was first used by Dr. Robert Stoller.

14. Patricia Albjerg Graham, "Women in Academe," *Science*, September 1970, p. 1286.

15. I first read Margaret Hennig's work, "Career Development for Women Executives" as an unpublished doctoral thesis for the Harvard School of Business Administration, September, 1970. Part of it has since been published in Margaret Hennig and Anne Jardim, *The Managerial Woman* (Garden City: Anchor Press, 1977), Part II.

16. Hennig and Jardim, *The Managerial Woman*, references on pp. 82, 86, 91, 92, 99.

17. For the way in which Orthodox Jewish beliefs about women affect national policies, see Lesley Hazelton, *Israeli Women: The Reality Behind the Myth* (New York: Simon & Schuster, 1977).

18. Dorothee Soelle, *Suffering*, trans. Everett R. Kalin (Philadelphia: Fortress Press, 1975), pp. 97–98. It is important to emphasize that Soelle's book is *not* concerned with women; the application of her thesis to women is mine.

19. *Ibid.*, p. 12.

20. *Ibid.*, p. 74.

21. *Ibid.*, pp. 13–14.

22. Adrienne Rich, *Women and Honor: Some Notes on Lying* (Pittsburgh: Motheroot Publications, 1977).

Notes to Chapter 3—

Women Writers and Female Characters: The Failure of Imagination (pp. *71* to *92*)

1. Simone de Beauvoir, *Force of Circumstance,* trans. Richard Howard (New York: G.P. Putnam's Sons, 1965), p. 268.

2. Maurice Beebe, *Ivory Towers and Sacred Founts* (New York: New York University Press, 1964), p. 99.

3. Patricia Beer, *Reader, I Married Him* (New York: Harper & Row, 1974), p. 181.

4. Cynthia Griffin Wolff, *A Feast of Words: The Triumph of Edith Wharton* (New York: Oxford University Press, 1977), pp. 9, 258, 256, 256. Emphasis is Wolff's.

5. Diana Trilling, "The Image of Woman in Contemporary Literature," *The Woman in America,* ed. Robert J. Lifton (Boston: Beacon Press, 1967), p. 65.

6. Susan Sontag, *Partisan Review,* Spring 1973, p. 206. Here she wrote: "The first responsibility of a 'liberated' woman is to lead the fullest, freest and most imaginative life she can. The second responsibility is her solidarity with other women. She may live and work and make love with men. But she has no right to represent her situation as simpler, or less suspect, or less full of compromises than it really is. Her good relations with men must not be bought at the price of betraying her sisters."

7. Doris Langley Moore, *E. Nesbit: A Biography* (New York: Chilton Books, 1966), p. 178.

8. This observation was made to me by Mortimer herself, in conversation in Cambridge, Mass.

9. Pauline Kael, *The New Yorker,* 10 October 1977, pp. 100–1.

10. Helene Moglen, *Charlotte Brontë: The Self Conceived* (New York:

W.W. Norton, 1976), p. 52. Moglen's book is one of the few biographies of women which deals with the problem of creating a self, and other vital feminist issues.

11. John E. Mack, *A Prince of Our Disorder: The Life of T.E. Lawrence* (Boston: Little, Brown, 1976), pp. 442–3.

12. Diane Johnson, *New York Review of Books,* 25 November 1976, p. 41.

13. Catharine Stimpson, "The Mind, the Body, and Gertrude Stein," *Critical Inquiry,* Spring 1977, p. 497.

14. Ann Douglas, *The Feminization of American Culture* (New York: Alfred A. Knopf, 1977), p. 44.

15. Aileen Kelly, *New York Review of Books,* 26 January 1978, pp. 28, 31. Emphasis is mine.

16. Adrienne Rich, "Three Conversations," *Adrienne Rich's Poetry,* ed. Barbara Charlesworth Gelpi and Albert Gelpi (New York: W.W. Norton, 1975), pp. 114–15. Ellin Sarot first brought to my attention the way in which women poets differ from women novelists. See my further discussion of Rich on women poets below, Chapter 5.

17. Bell Gale Chevigny, *The Woman and the Myth: Margaret Fuller's Life and Writings* (Old Westbury, N.Y.: The Feminist Press, 1976), p. 216.

Notes to Chapter 4—

Search for a Model: Female Childhood (pp. *93* to *124*)

1. Ellen Moers, *Literary Women* (Garden City: Doubleday, 1976) is particularly valuable for its discussion of the ways in which women writers, who may never have met, learned from and relied upon one another. Moers's work is also important in indicating the degree of control women writers did, in fact, manage to retain over their own lives.

2. Roy Schafer, "Problems in Freud's Psychology of Women," *Journal of the American Psychoanalytic Association,* vol. 22, no. 3 (1974).

3. Juliet Mitchell, *Psychoanalysis and Feminism* (New York: Vintage Books, 1975).

4. Sherry Ortner, *Feminist Studies*, vol. 2, no. 2/3 (1975), pp. 180–1, 179.

5. Dorothy Dinnerstein, *The Mermaid and the Minotaur* (New York: Harper & Row, 1976).

6. See Robert J. Stoller, *Sex and Gender* (New York: Jason Aronson, 1968). Stoller coined the phrase "core gender identity," which must be distinguished from gender: male homosexuals and transvestites have an especially strong "core gender identity." For studies in sex assignment, see J. Money and A.A. Ehrhardt, *Man and Woman, Boy and Girl* (Baltimore: Johns Hopkins University Press, 1973). A clear account of some of these developments can be found in Ethel Person, "Some New Observations on the Origins of Femininity," in Jean Strouse, ed., *Women and Analysis* (New York: Grossman, 1974), pp. 250–261. I am particularly indebted to Dr. Ethel Person, who first introduced me to much of the literature in this field, but who is not, of course, responsible for anything I have said about it.

7. The earliest account of this I know is in Ralph R. Greenson, "Dis-identifying from Mother: Its Special Importance for the Boy," in *International Journal of Psychoanalysis*, vol. 43 (1968), pp. 370–74.

8. Robert J. Stoller, *Perversion* (New York: Pantheon, 1975), p. 18.

9. See Jeanne Humphrey Block, "Conceptions of Sex Role: Some Cross-Cultural and Longitudinal Perspectives," *American Psychologist*, vol. 28, no. 6 (June 1973), pp. 512–526.

10. See Elizabeth A. Ashburn, *Motivation, Personality, and Work-Related Characteristics of Women in Male-Dominated Professions* (Washington, D.C.: National Association for Women Deans, Administrators, and Counselors, 1977).

11. *Ibid.*, p. 6.

12. Quoted in *Anaïs Nin: A Woman Speaks*, ed. Evelyn J. Hinz (Chicago: The Swallow Press, 1975), p. 229.

13. Kathleen Coburn, *In Pursuit of Coleridge* (London: Bodley Head, 1977), p. 11.

14. Helene Deutsch, *Confrontations with Myself* (New York: W.W. Norton, 1973), pp. 38, 39. Deutsch's only brother was not considered

clever enough to remain a Jew, and his father had him baptised as a Christian so that he might enter the Civil Service, p. 37.

15. *Ibid.*, p. 69.

16. Cheryl Crawford, *One Naked Individual: My Fifty Years in the Theatre* (Indianapolis: Bobbs-Merrill, 1977), p. 8.

17. *Ibid.*, p. 109.

18. Anne Roiphe, *New York Times Magazine*, 13 February 1972.

19. Golda Meir, *My Life* (New York: G.P. Putnam's Sons, 1975), p. 21.

20. Oriana Fallaci, *Interview with History* (New York: Liveright, 1976), p. 112.

21. *Ibid.*, pp. 112–13, 114.

22. I am grateful to Myra Jehlen for ideas about the ways in which women create themselves as novels.

23. Fallaci, *Interview with History*, p. 156.

24. *Ibid.*, pp. 171, 172–3.

25. For an autobiography of an Indian woman who early rebelled against the conventional female destiny, see Urmila Haksar, *The Future that Was* (New Delhi: Allied Publishers Private, 1973).

26. Arthur H. Nethercot, *The Last Four Lives of Annie Besant* (Chicago: University of Chicago Press, 1963), p. 76.

27. Freud also did not believe that Shakespeare wrote Shakespeare's plays.

28. Simone de Beauvoir, *Force of Circumstance*, p. 193.

29. Minutes of the October 20, 1977 meeting, Study Group on Women: Work and Personality in the Middle Years, Heller School, Brandeis University.

30. Simone de Beauvoir, *Memoirs of a Dutiful Daughter*, trans. James Kirkup (Baltimore, Penguin, 1963), p. 340.

31. I have taken the information about Schlafly from an article by Toni Carabillo in the *National NOW Times*, December 1977, pp. 8–9.

32. George Martin, *Madam Secretary: Frances Perkins* (Boston: Houghton Mifflin, 1976), p. 44.

33. *Ibid.*, pp. 195, 370, 206, 326.

34. *Beyond Sex-Role Stereotypes: Readings Toward a Psychology of Androgyny*, ed. Alexandra G. Kaplan and Joan P. Bean (Boston: Little, Brown, 1976), pp. 297, 330.

35. Frances Newman, *The Hardboiled Virgin*, quoted in Anne Firor Scott, *The Southern Lady: From Pedestal to Politics 1830–1930* (Chicago: University of Chicago Press, 1970), p. 224.

36. Naomi Mitchison, *Small Talk: Memories of an Edwardian Childhood* (London: Bodley Head, 1973).

37. There have been many studies of those factors which tend to produce achieving women. For an excellent summary of this work, and of the data which lie behind many of my statements, see Rosalind Barnett and Grace Baruch, *The Competent Woman: Perspectives on Development* (New York: Irvington-Halstead Press, 1978). The bibliography in this book names many of the studies on which I have relied.

38. Tom F. Driver, *Patterns of Grace: Human Experience as Word of God* (San Francisco: Harper & Row, 1977), p. 134.

Notes to Chapter 5—

Search for a Model: History and Literature (pp. *125* to *170*)

1. Lionel Trilling, *Sincerity and Authenticity* (Cambridge, Mass.: Harvard University Press, 1972), p. 1.

2. Lionel Trilling, *Beyond Culture* (New York: The Viking Press, 1965), p. 3.

3. William Gibson, *A Season in Heaven* (New York: Atheneum, 1974), p. 46.

4. *Columbia Spectator*, 7 June 1972.

5. Trilling, *Beyond Culture*, p. 8.

6. Lionel Trilling, *The Opposing Self* (New York: The Viking Press,

1955), p. 117. Both Irving Howe and Leon Edel have convincingly contradicted Trilling's interpretation of the novel.

7. For an account of Columbia's anti-Semitism before World War II, see Mortimer Adler, *Philosopher at Large* (New York: Macmillan, 1977), pp. 72–3. See also Lionel Trilling, "Young in the Thirties," *Commentary*, May 1966, p. 47.

8. Trilling, *Beyond Culture*, p. 13.

9. Trilling, *The Opposing Self*, pp. x, xiv.

10. Trilling, *Sincerity and Authenticity*, pp. 67, 66, 25.

11. *Ibid.*, pp. 35, 36, 37.

12. *Ibid.*, pp. 11, 42, 50.

13. *Ibid.*, p. 82.

14. *Ibid.*, pp. 85, 87, 92, 172.

15. Lionel Trilling, *The Liberal Imagination* (New York: The Viking Press, 1951), p. 148.

16. Patricia Meyer Spacks, ed., *Contemporary Women Novelists* (Englewood Cliffs, N.J.: Prentice-Hall, 1977), p. 14.

17. *Ibid.*, p. 133.

18. Erich Neumann, *Amor and Psyche: The Psychic Development of the Feminine*, trans. Ralph Manheim (Princeton: Princeton University Press, 1956).

19. Jean Hagstrum, "Eros and Psyche: Some Versions of Romantic Love and Delicacy," *Critical Inquiry*, Spring 1977, p. 527.

20. *Ibid.*, p. 534.

21. Neumann, pp. 113, 123.

22. *Ibid.*, pp. 71, 81, 85, 135.

23. Anne Sexton, *Transformations* (Boston: Houghton Mifflin, 1971), p. 54.

24. Bruno Bettelheim, *The Uses of Enchantment* (New York: Vintage Books 1977), p. 257.

25. Karen Rowe, "Feminism and Fairy Tales," Radcliffe Institute Working Paper, 1 March 1978, pp. 8, 12, 19, 20.

26. Bettelheim, *The Uses of Enchantment*, pp. 139, 17.

27. V. Propp, *Morphology of the Folktale* (Austin: University of Texas Press, 1975), pp. 79–80.

28. Bell Gale Chevigny, *The Woman and the Myth: Margaret Fuller's Life and Writings*, p. 264.

29. Sandra Gilbert, " 'My Name is Darkness': The Poetry of Self-Definition," *Contemporary Literature*, August 1977, pp. 446, 448, 456.

30. Froma Zeitlin, "The Dynamics of Misogyny: Myth and Mythmaking in the *Oresteia* of Aeschylus," Paper presented to the Columbia University Seminar on Women and Society, 19 December 1977.

31. Richard Kuhns, *The House, the City and the Judge: The Growth of Moral Awareness in The Oresteia* (Indianapolis: Bobbs-Merrill, 1962), p. 36.

32. Sarah B. Pomeroy, *Goddesses, Whores, Wives, and Slaves: Women in Classical Antiquity* (New York: Schocken Books, 1975), p. 4.

33. Zeitlin, "The Dynamics of Misogyny," p. 14.

34. Jane Harrison, *Prolegomena to the Study of Greek Religion* (New York: Meridian, 1959), p. 251.

35. H.D.F. Kitto, *Greek Tragedy* (Garden City, N.Y.: Anchor Books, 1954), p. 98.

36. Zeitlin, "The Dynamics of Misogyny," pp. 16, 19, 30.

37. Jane Harrison, *Themis* (Cleveland: Meridian, 1962) p. 271. Anne Barstow suggested to me the significance for modern women of this myth. Notice its importance in interpreting to the return of Isabel Archer to Pansy at the end of Henry James's *Portrait of a Lady*.

38. *Ibid.*, p. 273.

39. Linda Gordon, *Woman's Body, Woman's Right: A Social History of Birth Control in America* (New York: Penguin Books, 1977), pp. 9, 10, 11, 405–6. *Of Woman Born*, by Adrienne Rich, is a crucial book in this connection.

40. Kuhns, *The House, the City and the Judge*, pp. 29, 31.

41. George Thomson, *Aeschylus and Athens* (New York: Grosset & Dunlap, 1968), p. 271.

42. Zeitlin, "The Dynamics of Misogyny," p. 12.

43. Robert Graves, *The White Goddess* (New York: Vintage Books, 1958), p. 500.

44. Chevigny, *The Woman and The Myth*, p. 263.

45. Nancy Hale, *Mary Cassatt* (New York: Doubleday, 1975), p. 34.

46. Adrienne Rich, "Vesuvius at Home: The Power of Emily Dickinson," *Parnassus*, vol. 5, no. 1 (Fall/Winter 1976), pp. 59, 52, 56.

47. *Ibid.*, p. 62.

48. Iris Murdoch, *The Sovereignty of Good* (London: Routledge & Kegan Paul, 1970), pp. 66–67.

49. Joanne Feit Diehl, "Come Slowly—Eden; An Exploration of Women Poets and Their Muse," *Signs*, vol. 3, no. 3 (Spring, 1978), p. 574.

50. *Ibid.*, pp. 576, 577.

51. Rich, "Vesuvius at Home," pp. 66, 53.

Notes to Chapter 6—

Marriage and Family (pp. *171* to *197*)

1. Marilyn French, *The Women's Room* (New York: Summit Books, 1977), p. 193.

2. Quoted in Patricia Thomson, *George Sand and the Victorians* (New York: Columbia University Press, 1977), p. 69.

3. Doris Lessing, *The Golden Notebook* (New York: Simon & Schuster, 1962), p. 415.

4. Ronald Blythe, Introduction to *Emma* by Jane Austen (Middlesex, England: Penguin Books, 1966), p. 30.

5. Irving Howe, Introduction to *Jude the Obscure* by Thomas Hardy (Boston: Houghton Mifflin, 1965), pp. vi–vii. Howe points out that the Parnell case also forced a discussion of "the realities of the conjugal life."

6. *New York Times*, 7 February 1975; quoted in Signe Hammer, *Daughters & Mothers: Mothers & Daughters* (New York: Quadrangle Books, 1975).

7. James Dickey, review of *All My Pretty Ones*, *New York Times Book Review*, 28 April 1963; quoted in *Anne Sexton, A Self-Portrait in Letters*, ed. Linda Gray Sexton and Lois Aimes (Boston: Houghton Mifflin, 1977), p. 166.

8. *Ibid.*

9. Christopher Lasch, "The Narcissist Society," *New York Review of Books*, 30 September 1976, pp. 5–13.

10. Christopher Lasch, "Planned Obsolescence," *New York Review of Books*, 28 October 1976, p. 7.

11. Drs. Malkah Notman and Carol Gilligan do not believe that this period should be identified as adolescence. Their arguments are cogent, but I refer only to rather superficial similarities in the two stages. Minutes, Study Group on Women: Work and Personality in the Middle Years, Heller School, Brandeis University.

12. This idea was suggested by John G. Cawelti, *Adventure, Mystery and Romance* (Chicago: University of Chicago Press, 1976), p. 16.

13. H.G. Wells, *Experiment in Autobiography;* quoted in John Rosenberg, *Dorothy Richardson* (New York: Alfred A. Knopf, 1973), p. 44.

14. Howe, *World of Our Fathers*, p. 271. Ann Douglas, in *The Feminization of American Culture*, p. 77 explains the lack of woman's domestic solitude: "in mid-nineteenth-century America, women . . . were not merely denied private rooms: they denied themselves. Given their cultural isolation, a demand for a room of their own would seem like further renunciation of an already slender claim on life, acceptance of solitary confinement."

15. Woolf, *Three Guineas*, p. 218.

16. Nigel Nicolson and Joanne Trautman, eds., *The Letters of Virginia*

NOTES 225

Woolf, Vol. II (New York: Harcourt Brace Jovanovich, 1976), p. 599.

17. Barbara Raskin, *Loose Ends* (New York: Bantam Books, 1973), p. 1.

18. *Ibid.,* p. 3.

19. Quoted in Cheryl Walker, "American Women Poets: A Room of Their Own," Radcliffe Institute Working Paper, 1978, p. 8.

20. Norman Donaldson, Introduction to Mary Elizabeth Braddon, *Lady Audley's Secret* (New York: Dover, 1974), p. xiii. See also Mrs. Gaskell's complaint to Eliot Norton about similar conditions in *The Letters of Mrs. Gaskell,* ed. J.A.V. Chapple and Arthur Pollard (Cambridge, Mass.: Harvard University Press, 1967), p. 489. Phyllis Chesler reminds us that little has changed in over a century: "Most children in contemporary American culture invade their mothers' privacy, life space, sanity and selves to such an extent that she must give up these things in order not to commit violence. (Invasion of a boundary into deserted territory is perhaps less painful than one into occupied and functional territory. . . .)" Phyllis Chesler, *Women and Madness* (New York: Avon Books, 1972), p. 294.

21. Reprinted in Gerda Lerner, *The Female Experience* (Indianapolis: Bobbs-Merrill, 1977), p. 10.

22. James Woodress, in *Willa Cather: Her Life and Art* (Lincoln: University of Nebraska Press, 1970), p. 38, describes Cather's and Thea's rooms as identical.

23. Bobbie Ann Mason, *The Girl Sleuth* (Old Westbury, N.Y.: The Feminist Press, 1975), p. 78.

24. *New York Times Book Review,* 11 September 1977.

25. Michael Holroyd, *Hugh Kingsmill* (London: The Unicorn Press, 1964), p. 125.

26. Doris Lessing, "To Room 19," *A Man and Two Women and Other Stories* (New York: Simon & Schuster, 1963), pp. 297, 295, 311.

27. Gillian Martin, *The Goat, the Wolf, and the Crab* (New York: Charles Scribner's Sons, 1977), pp. 4–5.

28. Raskin, *Loose Ends,* pp. 312–13.

29. Chevigny, *The Woman and the Myth: Margaret Fuller's Life and Writings,* p. 277.

30. Sylvia Plath, *Letters Home,* ed. Aurelia Schosber Plath (New York: Harper & Row, 1975), p. 297.

31. Hanna Papanek, "Men, Women, and Work: Reflections on the Two-Person Career," *Changing Women in a Changing Society,* ed. Joan Huber (Chicago: University of Chicago Press, 1973), p. 100.

32. Dorothy Z. Ullian, "Masculinity & Femininity: A Childhood Perspective," Paper delivered at the National Council of Family Relations, October 22, 1976.

33. Richard P. Brickner, *My Second Twenty Years* (New York: Basic Books, 1976).

34. See, for example, Mary Jane Sherfey, *The Nature & Evolution of Female Sexuality* (New York: Vintage Books, 1973); Shere Hite, *The Hite Report* (New York: Macmillan, 1976).

35. There have been several recent, excellent studies of Alcott and her work: The essay on *Little Women* in Nina Auerbach, *Communities of Women: An Idea in Fiction* (Cambridge, Mass.: Harvard University Press, 1978); the Introduction to *Work,* by Sarah Elbert (New York: Schocken Books, 1977); the introduction to *Behind the Mask* and *Plots and Counterplots,* collections of the unknown thrillers of Alcott, by Madeleine Stern (New York: Bantam Books, 1978). *Louisa May: A Modern Biography of Louisa May Alcott,* by Martha Saxton (Boston: Houghton Mifflin, 1977) is conventional in its interpretation of the impulses to female action.

36. Chodorow, *The Reproduction of Mothering: Psychoanalysis and the Sociology of Gender,* p. 157.

37. See Elizabeth Janeway, "On 'Female Sexuality,' " *Women & Analysis,* ed. Jean Strouse (New York: Grossman Publishers, 1974), p. 59.

38. Chodorow, p. 167.

39. *Ibid.,* p. 169.

40. Rhona & Robert N. Rapoport, *Dual-Career Families Re-examined* (New York: Harper Colophon Books, 1976).

41. *Ibid.*, p. 9. The Rapoport revised edition points out, among much else of value, that the concept of Dual-Career families as "elite," because requiring help in the home, is not a viable conclusion. They have discovered that "life style" is a far likelier indication of similarity between families than class (an observation my experience strongly affirms).

42. *Ibid.*, p. 346.

43. *Ibid.*, p. 337.

44. Rabbi Burnam in Buber's *Tales of the Hasidim;* quoted in Soelle, *Suffering.*

45. Hebrews 7:18–19; quoted in Carter Heyward, *A Priest Forever* (New York: Harper & Row, 1976).

Notes to Chapter 7—

The Claims of Woman (pp. *199* to *212*)

1. *Time,* 1 May 1978.

2. Adrienne Rich, *The Dream of a Common Language* (New York: W. W. Norton, 1978).

3. *Art, Politics, and Will: Essays in Honor of Lionel Trilling,* ed. Quentin Anderson, Stephen Donadio, and Steven Marcus (New York: Basic Books, 1977), pp. 173–190.

4. *Ibid.*, pp. 252, 218.

5. *Wellesley Alumnae Magazine,* vol. 62, no. 2 (Winter 1978). The entire issue was devoted to volunteerism. President Newell's speech, pp. 6–7.

6. Louise Bogan, "From the Journals of a Poet," *The New Yorker,* 30 January 1978, p. 62.

7. The most famous exposition of this theory is Alice Rossi, "A Biosocial Perspective on Parenting," *Daedalus,* Spring, 1977. For criticisms of Rossi's position, see Chodorow; Wini Breines, Margaret Cerullo, Judith Stacey, "Social Biology, Family Studies, and Antifeminist Backlash," in *Feminist Studies,* vol. 4, no. 1 (February 1978).

8. Yolanda and Robert F. Murphy, *Women of the Forest* (New York: Columbia University Press, 1974).

9. From the Durham collection in the Royal Anthropological Institute. The account apparently describes a photo taken by Durham, "A virgin of the Klementi tribe."

10. See Auerbach, *Communities of Women,* pp. 55–73.

Selective Bibliography

In this bibliography I take it for granted that the reader, like myself, will have read and made part of herself (or himself) the works that are fundamental to contemporary feminism: those by Friedan, Millett, Greer, Janeway, Gornick, and others. Their absence here emphasizes, I hope, their importance at another stage of feminism. What remain in this bibliography are works which may help a committed or interested feminist in the process of reinvention. I have not included books by nonfeminist authors even though they are discussed in the text. Each reader will, I trust, be able to provide her or his own list of nonfeminist writings which, when reinterpreted, now speak persuasively to women.

The texts I list are the ones I know. Others, surely, could add titles no less important than these. I am, however, convinced that these works, if not the only or best examples I might have chosen, will in any case lead the reader to sources equally good or better. I have occasionally listed unpublished materials, in part because I believe that their authors will soon be published, and should be watched out for, but also because I could not find their ideas so well expressed elsewhere. Finally, I have listed, in a separate category, those collections so rich in important articles that one or two cannot be selected out. These collections make a fine starting place, and contain essays by important scholars who may not be individually mentioned in the bibliography.

Ashburn, Elizabeth A. *Motivation, Personality, and Work-Related Characteristics of Women in Male-Dominated Professions.* Washington: National Association for Women Deans, Administrators, and Counselors, 1977.

Auerbach, Nina. *Communities of Women: An Idea in Fiction.* Cambridge, Mass.: Harvard University Press, 1978.

Barnett, Rosalind, and Baruch, Grace. *The Competent Woman: Perspectives on Development.* New York: Irvington-Halstead, 1978.

Bart, Pauline B., and Grossman, Marlyn. "Menopause." In *The Woman Patient,* edited by Carol Nadelson and Malkah T. Notman. New York: Plenum Press, 1978.

Beauvoir, Simone de. *The Second Sex.* Translated by H. M. Parshley. New York: Knopf, 1957.

———. *Memoirs of a Dutiful Daughter.* Translated by James Kirkup. 1959; reprint ed., Baltimore: Penguin, 1963.

———. *Force of Circumstance.* Translated by Richard Howard. New York: G. P. Putnam's Sons, 1965.

Beer, Patricia. *Reader, I Married Him: A Study of the Women Characters of Jane Austen, Charlotte Brontë, Elizabeth Gaskell and George Eliot.* New York: Barnes & Noble, 1974.

Bell, Susan Groag. *Women in History Who Began Careers in Middle Age.* Unpublished monograph, August, 1969.

Bernard, Jesse. *The Future of Marriage.* New York: Bantam, 1973.

———. *The Future of Motherhood.* New York: Penguin, 1974.

Blanchard, Paula. *Margaret Fuller: From Transcendentalism to Revolution.* New York: Delacorte Press, 1978.

Chafe, William. *The American Woman: Her Changing Social, Economic, and Political Roles, 1920–1970.* New York: Oxford University Press, 1972.

———. *Women and Equality.* New York: Oxford University Press, 1977.

Chesler, Phyllis. *Women and Madness.* New York: Avon, 1972.

Chevigny, Bell Gale. *The Woman and the Myth: Margaret Fuller's Life and Writings.* Old Westbury, N.Y.: The Feminist Press, 1976.

Chicago, Judy. *Through the Flower: My Struggle as a Woman Artist.* Garden City, N.Y.: Doubleday, 1977.

Chodorow, Nancy. *The Reproduction of Mothering: Psychoanalysis and the Sociology of Gender.* Berkeley: University of California Press, 1978.

Cott, Nancy F. *The Bonds of Womanhood: "Woman's Sphere" in New England, 1780–1835.* New Haven: Yale University Press, 1977.

Degler, Carl. Introduction to *Women and Economics,* by Charlotte Perkins Gilman. New York: Harper & Row, 1966, pp. vi–xxxv.

Deutsch, Helene. *Confrontations with Myself.* New York: Norton, 1973.

Dinnerstein, Dorothy. *The Mermaid and the Minotaur: Sexual Arrangements and Human Malaise.* New York: Harper & Row, 1976.

Driver, Tom F. *Patterns of Grace: Human Experience as Word of God.* San Francisco: Harper & Row, 1977.

Dubois, Barbara. "Feminist Perspectives on Psychotherapy and the Psychology of Women: An Exploratory Study in the Development of Clinical Theory." Ph.D. dissertation, Harvard University, 1976.

DuPlessis, Rachel Blau. "The Critique of Consciousness and Myth in Levertov, Rich and Rukeyser." *Feminist Studies* 3 (1975):199–221.

Gelfant, Blanche. "Reconsideration: *The Mountain Lion* by Jean Stafford." *New Republic*, 10 May 1975, pp. 22–25.

Gilligan, Carol. "In a Different Voice: Women's Conception of Morality." Unpublished monograph, Harvard University, 1977.

Gilman, Charlotte Perkins. *The Living of Charlotte Perkins Gilman: An Autobiography.* 1935; reprint ed., New York: Harper & Row, 1975.

Gordon, Linda. *Woman's Body, Woman's Right: A Social History of Birth Control in America.* New York: Penguin, 1977.

Harris, Ann Sutherland, and Nochlin, Linda. *Women Artists: 1550–1950.* New York: Knopf, 1977.

Hawkes, Ellen. "A Form of One's Own." *Mosaic* 8 (1974):-77–90.

Hazelton, Lesley. *Israeli Women: The Reality Behind the Myth.* New York: Simon & Schuster, 1977.

Helson, Ravena. "The Changing Image of the Career Woman." *Journal of Social Issues* 28 (1972):33–46.

Hennig, Margaret. "Career Development for Women Executives." Ph.D. dissertation, Harvard Business School, 1970.

———, and Jardim, Anne. *The Managerial Woman.* Garden City, N.Y.: Doubleday, 1977.

Heyward, Carter. *A Priest Forever: The Formation of a Woman and a Priest.* New York: Harper & Row, 1976.

Huber, Joan; Rexroat, Cynthia; and Spitze, Glenna. *ERA in Illinois: A Crucible of Opinion on Women's Status.* Department of Sociology, University of Illinois at Urbana-Champaign, 1976.

Lerner, Gerda. *The Female Experience: An American Documentary.* Indianapolis: Bobbs-Merrill, 1977.

Lever, Janet. "Sex Differences in Games Children Play." *Social Problems* 23 (1976):478–487.

Levine, James A. *Who Will Raise the Children? New Options for Fathers (and Mothers)*. New York: Bantam, 1977.

Maslow, Abraham H. *Toward a Psychology of Being*. New York: Van Nostrand, 1968.

———. *Motivation and Personality*. New York: Harper & Row, 1970.

Miller, Jean Baker. *Toward a New Psychology of Women*. Boston: Beacon Press, 1976.

Moers, Ellen. *Literary Women: The Great Writers*. Garden City, N.Y.: Doubleday, 1976.

Moglen, Helene. *Charlotte Brontë: The Self Conceived*. New York: Norton, 1976.

Moorehead, Caroline. "A Talk with Simone de Beauvoir." *New York Times Magazine*, 2 June 1974, pp. 16–22.

Neumann, Erich. *Amor and Psyche: The Psychic Development of the Feminine. A Commentary on the Tale by Apuleius*. Translated by Ralph Manheim. Princeton: Princeton University Press, 1956.

O'Neill, William L. *Everyone Was Brave: A History of Feminism in America*. Chicago: Quadrangle Books, 1971.

Ortner, Sherry B. "Is Female to Male as Nature Is to Culture?" In *Women, Culture, and Society*, edited by Michelle Zimbalist Rosaldo and Louise Lamphere, pp. 67–87. Stanford: Stanford University Press, 1974.

———. "Oedipal Father, Mother's Brother, and the Penis: A Review of Juliet Mitchell's *Psychoanalysis and Feminism*." *Feminist Studies* 2 (1975):167–182.

Ozick, Cynthia. "Women and Creativity: The Demise of the Dancing Dog." In *Woman in Sexist Society: Studies in Power and Powerlessness*, edited by Vivian Gornick and Barbara K. Moran, pp. 431–451. New York: Signet, 1972.

Perlmutter, Morton S. "The Frail-Male Syndrome." Unpublished paper, School of Social Work, University of Wisconsin–Madison, 1974.

Rapoport, Rhona, and Rapoport, Robert. *Dual-Career Families Re-examined: New Integrations of Work and Family.* New York: Harper & Row, 1976.

Rich, Adrienne. *Poems: Selected and New, 1950–1974.* New York: Norton, 1975.

————. *Adrienne Rich's Poetry: Texts of the Poems. The Poet on Her Work. Reviews and Criticism.* Edited by Barbara Charlesworth Gelpi and Albert Gelpi. New York: Norton, 1975.

————. *Of Woman Born: Motherhood as Experience and Institution.* New York: Norton, 1976.

————. "Vesuvius at Home: The Power of Emily Dickinson." *Parnassus* 5 (1976):49–74.

————. *The Dream of a Common Language: Poems 1974–1977.* New York: Norton, 1978.

Rose, Phyllis. *Woman of Letters: A Life of Virginia Woolf.* New York: Oxford University Press, 1978.

Rossi, Alice. "Equality Between the Sexes: An Immodest Proposal." In *The Woman in America,* edited by Robert Jay Lifton, pp. 98–143. Boston: Beacon Press, 1965.

————. "Sex Equality: The Beginning of Ideology." In *Masculine/Feminine,* edited by Betty Roszak and Theodore Roszak, pp. 173–185. New York: Harper & Row, 1969.

Rowe, Karen E. "Feminism and Fairy Tales." Radcliffe Institute Working Paper, Cambridge, Mass., 1978.

Schafer, Roy. "Problems in Freud's Psychology of Women." *Journal of the American Psychoanalytic Association* 22 (1974):-459–485.

Sherfey, Mary Jane. *The Nature & Evolution of Female Sexuality.* New York: Vintage, 1973.

Smedley, Agnes. *Daughter of Earth.* 1929, reprint ed., Old Westbury, N.Y.: The Feminist Press, 1976.

Smith-Rosenberg, Carroll. "The Female World of Love and Ritual: Relations between Women in Nineteenth-Century America." *Signs* 1 (1975):1–30.

Spacks, Patricia. "Women's Stories, Women's Selves." *Hudson Review* 30 (1977):29–46.

————. Introduction to *Contemporary Women Novelists*. Edited by Patricia Spacks. Englewood Cliffs, N.J.: Prentice-Hall, 1977.

Stimpson, Catharine R. "The Mind, the Body, and Gertrude Stein." *Critical Inquiry* 3 (1977):489–506.

Stone, Donald. "Victorian Feminism and the Nineteenth-Century Novel." *Women's Studies* 1 (1972):65–91.

Strachey, Ray. *The Cause: A Short History of the Women's Movement in Great Britain.* 1936; reprint ed., Port Washington, N.Y.: Kennikat Press, 1975.

Thomson, Patricia. *George Sand and the Victorians: Her Influence and Reputation in Nineteenth-Century England.* New York: Columbia University Press, 1977.

Ullian, Dorothy. "Bedfellows Make Strange Politics." Unpublished paper, Pioneers for Century III Conference, 1975.

————. "Masculinity and Femininity: A Childhood Perspective." Unpublished paper, National Council on Family Relations, 1976.

Walker, Cheryl. "American Women Poets: A Room of Their Own." Radcliffe Institute Working Paper, Cambridge, Mass., 1978.

Collections

Huber, Joan, ed. *Changing Women in a Changing Society.* Chicago: University of Chicago Press, 1973.

Kaplan, Alexandra G., and Bean, Joan P., eds. *Beyond Sex-Role Stereotypes: Readings Toward a Psychology of Androgyny.* Boston: Little, Brown, 1976.

Kundsin, Ruth B., ed. *Women and Success: The Anatomy of Achievement.* New York: Morrow, 1974.

Mednick, Martha Tamara Shuch; Tangri, Sandra Schwartz; and Hoffman, Lois W., eds. *Women and Achievement: Social and Motivational Analyses.* New York: Halsted Press (Wiley), 1975.

Miller, Jean Baker, ed. *Psychoanalysis and Women.* Baltimore: Penguin, 1973.

Ruddick, Sara, and Daniels, Pamela, eds. *Working It Out: 23 Women Writers, Artists, Scientists, and Scholars Talk About Their Lives and Work.* New York: Pantheon, 1977.

Strouse, Jean, ed. *Women & Analysis: Dialogues on Psychoanalytic Views of Femininity.* New York: Grossman, 1974.

Index

Adams, Robert, 199–200
Addams, Jane, 44
Adler, Mortimer, 221
"Albanian virgins," *see*
  Klementi
Alcott, Louisa May, 181–82
  Little Women, 190–91, 210–11,
  212
"Ancient Wisdom," 57, 60,
  115, 116
Androgyny, 62, 141–42, 158
Antigone, 110

Anxiety in women, 31, 101
Arendt, Hannah, 87–88
Athene, 163
  in the *Odyssey,* 40, 41
  in the *Oresteia,* 152–53, 155,
  158
Auden, W. H., 173
Auerbach, Nina, 226, 228
Austen, Jane, 66, 72, 135–36,
  170, 174
Autonomy, *see* Women,
  imagination, failure of

Bailey, Alice, 115
Barnett, Rosalind, 220
Barstow, Anne, 123, 222
Baruch, Grace, 213, 220
Beauvoir, Simone de, 72,
    116–18, 207
Beebe, Maurice, 80
Beer, Patricia, quoted, 81–82
Bell, Daniel, 200–202
Benedict, Ruth, 45
Ben-Gurion, David, 112
Besant, Annie, 114–15
Bettelheim, Bruno, 145, 147,
    149
Bible, quoted, 197
Black women, 23–24
Blacks, 27, 42
Blavatsky, Helena, 114, 115
Blythe, Ronald, 174
Bogan, Louise, 208
Bonheur, Rosa, 39, 43
Boston Globe, 27, 28
Bradden, Mary Elizabeth, 181,
    225
Breines, Wini, 227
Brontë, Charlotte, 84–85, 170
    The Professor, 172
Brontë, Emily, 170
Brown, Norman O., 142
Browning, Elizabeth Barrett,
    169–70
Bryant, Anita, 98, 196
Bryn Mawr College, 120
Buber, Martin, 132
    quoted, 197
Burnam, Rabbi (Buber's *Tales of
    the Hasidim*), 227

Carabillo, Toni, 219
Cassatt, Mary, 164

Cather, Willa, 182
    novels of, 79–81
Cawelti, John G., 224
Cerullo, Margaret, 227
Chesler, Phyllis, 225
Childbirth, 194–95
    adoption of child, 195
Chodorow, Nancy, 32, 102,
    189, 191–93, 196, 214
Chopin, Kate, 182
Cinderella, 144–46, 148
Coburn, Kathleen, 107–8
Columbia University, 22, 126,
    129, 130, 131, 203, 207,
    208
    tenured women, faculty of
    arts and sciences, 46–52,
    64–65, 207
Conservatives, opinions of,
    32–33, 88, 118–19, 156,
    159–60, 177
Cott, Nancy, 214
Cowley, Malcolm, 61, 62
Crawford, Cheryl, 109–10

Degas, Hilaire, 164
Demeter and Persephone, 156,
    160, 207, 222
Derida, Jacques, 209
Deutsch, Helene, 99, 101,
    108–9, 110, 111, 112,
    118–19, 155, 158, 218–19
Dickens, Charles, 37, 135
Dickey, James, 176
Dickinson, Emily, 91, 165–67,
    176–77, 180
    quoted, 167, 177
Dinnerstein, Dorothy, 102
Donaldson, Norman, 225
Donne, John, 167

Douglas, Ann, 217, 224
Drabble, Margaret, 28–29, 71–72
Driver, Tom F., 20, 123–24
Dual-Career Family, 193–95, 227
"symmetrical family," 196

Eddy, Mary Baker, 203
Elbert, Sarah, 226
Eliot, George, 81–82, 170, 173–74, 183
Middlemarch, 173
Eliot, T. S., 22
Ephron, Nora, 213
Episcopal Church, women priests in, 20, 24–25
Equal Rights Amendment, 88, 118, 120, 175
Eros and Psyche, 140–44, 146, 148

Fadiman, Clifton, 129
Fairy tales, 144–50
Fallaci, Oriana, 113
Family, 32, 33, 87, 105, 156, 159
father as full parent, 195, 196
restructuring of, 189–90, 191–97
Farnham, Marynia, 43
Father as girl's role model, 50, 52, 123
Female, see Women
Female development, 104–5
Feminism
denials of, 26, 27, 28, 208
French and American compared, 208–10

as strident, 205
younger faculty women and, 207
see also Women; Women's movement
Fiet Diehl, Joanne, 168
Fitzgerald, Robert, 41
Flaubert, Gustave, 149
Forster, E. M., 175
quoted, 95–96
Fox, Emmet, 60–61
French, Marilyn, The Women's Room, 40, 172
Freud, Sigmund, 32, 48, 58, 69, 96, 98, 100–102, 108, 119, 132, 145, 150, 161, 167, 172, 187, 191–92, 219
Freudian psychoanalysts, 98–99, 178
Friends of Columbia Libraries, 127–28
Fuller, Margaret, 86, 92, 150, 163, 185

Gandhi, Indira, 112–16
Gibson, William, 126
Gilbert, Sandra, 151
Gilligan, Carol, 224
Gilman, Charlotte Perkins, 15–16, 213
Giroud, Françoise, 44
Godwin, Gail, 90–91
Gordon, Linda, 161
Gould, Lois, 91
Gould, Roger, 116
Graham, Patricia Albjerg, 49
Graves, Robert, 163
Green, Martin, 149
Greenacre, Phyllis, 99
Grimm fairy tales, theme of

Grimm fairy tales *(continued)*
  "three brothers," 147–49
Gussow, Mel, 28

Hagstrum, Jean, 141–42
Haksar, Urmila, 219
Haldane, J. B. S., 122
Hale, Nancy, 164
Haley, Alex, *see Roots*
Hamilton, Alice, 39
Hammett, Dashiell, 84
Hardy, Thomas, 174–75
Harrison, Jane, 222
Harvard University, 27
Hawthorne, Nathaniel, 74
Hazelton, Lesley, 215
Hedda Gabler complex, 121–22
Hegel, Georg, 134
Heilbrun, Carolyn G.
  mother of, 16–17, 19, 52,
    55–58, 59, 65, 68–69
  father of, 19, 21, 52–55,
    58–59, 61–62, 115–16
Heilbrun, Margaret, 211
Hellman, Lillian, 84
Hennig, Margaret, 48, 49–51,
    109, 211
Heyward, Carter, 227
Hitler, Adolf, 23, 130
Holroyd, Michael, 225
Homer, 163, 169
Hopkins, Gerard Manley, 180
Horney, Karen, 94, 99, 110
Howe, Irving, 174–75, 224
  World of Our Fathers, 19, 21,
    173, 179

Ibsen, Henrik, 137
  Nora in *A Doll's House*, 178,
    179, 180

Imagination, *see* Women,
  imagination, failure of

James, Henry, 73, 74, 174, 175
  The Bostonians, 128–29
  Portrait of a Lady, 222
Janeway, Elizabeth, 226
Jehlen, Myra, 219
Jewish Theological Seminary,
    63–64
Jewishness
  consciousness of, 18–19, 20,
    22–23, 57, 60
  Jew as outsider, 37, 38, 41,
    61
  Anti-Semitism, 20, 23, 61,
    130
  Judaism and women, 21, 37,
    62, 109, 215
Johnson, Diane, 85
Joyce, James
  Finnegan's Wake, 200
  Leopold Bloom in *Ulysses*, 40,
    41, 62
  Molly Bloom in *Ulysses*,
    41–42
Jung, Carl, 43

Kael, Pauline, 83–84
Kelber, Mimi, 214
Kelly, Aileen, 89–90
Kingsmill, Hugh, 225
Kitto, H. D. F., 157
Klementi, 211, 228
Kuhns, Richard, 154, 162

Lacan, Jacques, 209
Lasch, Christopher, 177–78
Lattimore, Richard, 152
Lazareff, Helene, 44

League of Women Voters, 27
Lerner, Gerda, 225
Lessing, Doris
  Martha Quest, 139
  "To Room 19," 183
Levertov, Denise
  poetry quoted, 91–92, 124
Levi-Strauss, Claude, 150

Mack, John, 85
Male
  dysfunctions, 104
  "fragility," 185–89
  initiation rites, 104
  myths about women, 151,
    210
  role models, 31, 94–95,
    97–98, 140, 150, 151
  writers and autonomous
    women characters, 73–74
Manhood
  defined as *not* womanly, 33,
    192, 193
Markievicz, Con, 177
Marriage, 162, 172, 177–79,
  189
  in fiction, 171–77, 180–81
Martin, Gillian, *The Goat, the
  Wolf, and the Crab,* 183–84
Martin, George, 220
Martineau, Harriet, 43
Marx, Eleanor, 89–90
Mason, Bobby Ann, 182
Meir, Golda, 111–12, 113, 114
Mellown, Elgin, 139
Mentor, 51, 164
Meredith, George, 174
Michelet, Jules, 200
Mitchell, Juliet, 100–101
Mitchison, Naomi, 122

Moers, Ellen, 217
Moglen, Helene, 84–85, 217
Money, John, and Anke A.
  Ehrhardt, 218
Moore, Doris Langley, 216
Morrison, Toni, 182
Mortimer, Penelope, 83
Moslem religion, 64
Motherhood
  exalted, 119, 139, 159–60,
    161
  mother's ambivalence toward
    children, 16
  mothers of achieving women,
    121–22, 123
  "myth" of, in opposition to
    dual-career family, 194
Mount Holyoke College,
  119–20
Murdoch, Iris, 83, 167
Murphy, Yolande and Robert,
  210
Muses, 163, 169
  as male, 166–67
  for women, 163–67, 169, 170

Nehru, Jawaharlal, 112, 114–15
Nesbit, E., 83
Nethercot, Arthur, 219
New criticism, 22
Neumann, Erich, 141–44
Newman, Frances, 220
New York Times, 28
Niebuhr, Reinhold, 132
Nightingale, Florence, 43
Norton, Caroline, 43
Notman, Malkah, 224

Odysseus, 40–41, 164
Oedipus, 138–39

Oedipus complex, 101–103, 150, 191–93
Olsen, Tillie, 188
Oresteia, 152–60, 161
  Agamemnon, 153
  Aegisthus, 153
  Cassandra, 153
  Clytemnestra, 152, 153–54, 155
  Electra, 153, 154–55, 157, 163
  Erinyes/Eumenides, 153, 157–58
Ornitz, Samuel, 213
Ortner, Sherry, 101–2
Outsider
  see Jew as outsider; Women, as outsiders
Oxford Classical Dictionary, 169

Papenek, Hanna, 186–87
Penelope (in Odyssey), 40–41
Perkins, Frances, 43, 119–21
Person, Ethel, 218
Plath, Sylvia, 186
Pomeroy, Sarah, 155
Porter, Cole, 70
Potter, Beatrix, 84
Power (institutional, political), 199, 202–6
Propp, Vladimir, 149–50

Radcliffe Institute, 17, 26, 48, 188
Rapoport, Rhona and Robert, see Dual-Career Family
Raskin, Barbara, Loose Ends, 180–81, 182–83
Ray, Gordon, 128
Reformation, 25

Renault, Mary, novels of, 74–79
Rhodes Scholarships, Harvard women and, 27–28, 72, 112
Rhys, Jean, 139
Rich, Adrienne, 222
  desire for a son, 45, 124
  on Emily Dickinson, 165–66
  on poetry, 169–70
  poetry quoted, 52, 170, 199
  on women lying with their bodies, 70
  on women's "negative capability," 91
Roiphe, Anne, 219
Role models, see Father as girl's role model; Male, role models
Room of one's own
  as death, 183–84
  female concept, 179–83
Roots (by Alex Haley), 19
Rossi, Alice, 106, 227
Rousseau, Jean-Jacques, 133
Rowe, Karen, 146–47
Royal Anthropological Institute, 211, 228

Sartre, Jean-Paul, 116–18
Schafer, Roy, 100, 102
Schlafly, Phyllis, 43, 118–19, 159, 219–20
Schwartz, Maurice, 62
Selfhood, 85, 130–37, 201–2
Sexton, Anne, 176
  poetry quoted, 144–45, 176
Sexuality, 189, 194, 195–96
Shaw, George Bernard, 43
Sheehy, Gail, 178
Sidney, Sir Philip, 163, 164, 168

Sleeping Beauty, 145, 150
Smith-Rosenberg, Carroll,
 38–39, 214
Soelle, Dorothee, see Suffering
Sontag, Susan, 82–83, 216
Spacks, Patricia, 139
Stacey, Judith, 227
Stein, Gertrude, 62, 85–86
Stern, Madeleine, 226
Stimpson, Catharine, 85
Stoller, Robert, 105, 215,
 218
Strachey, Ray, 215
Suffering, 65–68, 215
Supreme Court (U.S.), 207

Telemachus (in *Odyssey*), 40, 41,
 164
Theosophy, 114
Thompson, Clara, 110
Thompson, Dorothy, 109–
 10
Thomson, George, 162
Thomson, Patricia, 223
Thoreau, Henry David, 92
Tiger, Lionel, 38, 214
Tillich, Paul, 132
Tocqueville, Alexis de, 33
Tokenism, 24, 42, 99, 112,
 120, 149
Trilling, Diana, 82, 129
Trilling, Lionel, 125–37,
 137–38, 177, 201
 memorial volume, 199, 200
The Trojan Women, 138
Twins, 191
Two-Person Career, 18,
 186–87, 193–94

Ulanov, Ann, 214
Ullian, Dorothy, 188

United Nations
 sexual harrassment of women
 working at, 25–26, 213

Walker, Cheryl, 225
Ward, Mrs. Humphrey, 43
Webb, Beatrice, 43
Webb, Sidney, 43
Weil, Simone, 69–70
Wellesley College, 18, 22, 60,
 61, 119
 president of on volunteerism,
 203, 227
Wells, H. G., 179
Wharton, Edith, 82
Wilson, Edmund, 106
Wolff, Cynthia, 82
Wollstonecraft, Mary, 45
Women
 achieving, in male-dominated
 professions, 106–23
 bonding with males (as
 "honorary men"), 24, 29,
 39, 43, 46, 47–48, 107,
 211–12
 despising of other women,
 43–45, 50
 fantasies of, 112, 124,
 167
 imagination, failure of, 26,
 30, 34, 71–74, 81–82,
 84–85
 as outsiders, 20, 30, 37–42,
 49, 70
 priests, see Episcopal Church
 sons, desire for, 45
 support systems, networks,
 26, 38–39
 see also, Father; Feminism;
 Motherhood; Selfhood;
 Tokenism

Women's movement
  cycles of, 24, 25, 26, 97,
    161
Woodham-Smith, Cecil, 225
Woodress, James, 225
Woolf, Virginia, 70, 179–80,
    208
  Jacob's Room, 185
  Society of Outsiders, 39–
    40

Wright, Richard, 70
Wylie, Elinor, 181

Yalow, Rosalyn, 199
Yeats, W. B., 22, 177
Yezierska, Anzia, Bread Givers,
    148

Zeitlin, Froma, 152, 156, 158